A LITTLE BIT

OF

PALMISTRY

A LITTLE BIT
OF
PALMISTRY

AN INTRODUCTION TO
PALM READING

CASSANDRA EASON

STERLING ETHOS
New York

STERLING ETHOS
New York

An Imprint of Sterling Publishing Co., Inc.
1166 Avenue of the Americas
New York, NY 10036

ISBN 978-1-4549-3225-3

Distributed in Canada by Sterling Publishing Co., Inc.
c/o Canadian Manda Group, 664 Annette Street
Toronto, Ontario M6S 2C8, Canada
Distributed in the United Kingdom by GMC Distribution Services
Castle Place, 166 High Street, Lewes, East Sussex BN7 1XU, England
Distributed in Australia by NewSouth Books
University of New South Wales, Sydney, NSW 2052, Australia

For information about custom editions, special sales, and premium and corporate purchases,
please contact Sterling Special Sales at 800-805-5489 or specialsales@sterlingpublishing.com.

Manufactured in the United States of America

4 6 8 10 9 7 5

sterlingpublishing.com

Interior design by Lorie Pagnozzi
Cover design by Elizabeth Mihaltse Lindy

Illustrations by Alexis Seabrook on pages xiv, xv, 4, 5, 9, 17, 18, 19, 22, 32, 34, 35,
36, 39, 41, 48, 49, 50, 51, 52, 54, 56, 57, 58, 59, 75, 83, 84, 85, 86, 87, 88, 89, 97,
Shutterstock.com pages iii, 1, 17, 31, 47, 65, 81, 97

CONTENTS

INTRODUCTION: WHAT IS PALMISTRY?

Palmistry is probably the most fun and most straightforward and exciting of all methods of divination. Yet many palmistry books are bought and abandoned a quarter of the way through because of their complexity, such as the hundreds of rules you apparently need to learn.

However, you can learn simple, but accurate, basic palmistry in a relatively short time with a minimum of rules, most of which are common sense, and so in this book I concentrate on the essentials, things that are necessary for accurate readings without destroying their spontaneity. Think of palmistry as a psychic art where you tune in to your subject's psyche via their palms, using what is basically psychometry or psychic touch.

We will practice this intuitive approach in Chapter 1, and later in more detail, where you can combine intuition with knowledge of what the lines and markings traditionally signify, thus gaining a full picture on all levels, not just based on outer physical signs.

THE POWER OF TOUCH

Lovers, as well as parents and children, hold hands. We use our hands to soothe others in distress by touching their hand gently; we also use them to make friendly initial connection with someone new, or whom we know formally, through a handshake. Through that handshake, we can often determine the level of trustworthiness of a person as our two energy fields make a connection. Palmistry involves this mingling of energy fields or auras of the reader and their subjects.

Use palmistry for reading the potentials of your child or teenager, having a fun palm-reading party with your friends (more on this later), or seeking the compatibilities between yourself and a loved one as your relationship evolves, and to answer the questions and dilemmas of yourself and others through discovering the potentials, opportunities, and challenges revealed in the hand.

WHERE TO START

Both hands can be read, though some readers, especially if time is short, focus on the main hand that is used for writing, referred to in palmistry as the "Active" hand, and this alone can record those opportunities and challenges in your present and future and so help to make informed choices.

The non-dominant hand, the one you don't use to write, is known as the "Inactive" hand, and reflects your potential, your treasure box of natural talents and weaknesses, and what you are thinking about doing in the longer term, or would like to do. The Active hand reveals what you are doing or planning on doing in the near future.

Hold the Inactive hand of a trusted friend or family member, using your Active hand, palm to palm, for a minute or two at a time when you will not be disturbed. This gentle but firm tactile contact is the essence of the best palm reading, as it is here that intuitive and telepathic connections are easily made. Now place their Inactive hand flat on a table, palm facing up.

Gently and slowly pass your downturned Active hand, fingers curved an inch or two (a few centimeters) above the palm of the Inactive hand of the subject. Firstly, move in circles over the whole palm and, if the connection is not strong, move your hand nearer if necessary, so it is almost touching the subject's palm. *Feel* the areas where the energies are strong but regular, areas that seem dead or blocked, and ones where the energies are harsh and very fast. You may get images in your mind, or hear words, or just gain impressions.

Now move the index finger of the hand you are using gently above the different lines and mounds of the subject's hand, and feel the relative energies. At the beginning of Chapter 1 is a diagram showing the names of these lines, but you may prefer to discover what you feel without knowledge getting in the way at this initial stage.

Using a copy of the blank hands at the end of this chapter, mark the energies by creating your own shorthand, perhaps a wavy line for naturally flowing energies, pale straight lines with breaks where you felt them for blocked energies, and dark zigzags for overly harsh energies.

Now change to the other hand, holding their Active hand for a minute or two, then placing that hand flat on the table but still using your own Active hand to assess the energies.

Afterward, compare the two hands and write down what you feel, and then you can discuss it with your subject, and the two of you can piece together the significance.

Date and store the image and, when you have learned the

conventional meanings by reading the subsequent chapters of this book, re-examine the original hand prints; you should find remarkable similarities in the results. (If this re-examination is more than three months after the initial assessment, or if major life events have occurred in the subject's life, the energies may be slightly different.)

ONGOING SELF-ASSESSMENT

The most effective case study is yourself, since each time you read a chapter, you can draw on your original diagrams.

Initially read your own palms intuitively as above, using your Active hand to assess your Inactive hand and your Inactive hand to assess your Active one. Again, date these and save them. As you read the chapters, you will learn the formal significance of a set of markings or lines; draw these on the diagrams of your hands. By the time you finish the book, you will have a very clear picture.

WHAT YOU NEED TO BEGIN PALMISTRY

You need remarkably little or nothing; and in time, as you encounter people at work or socially, you can almost instantly assess their hands—even the counter assistant at the checkout in the supermarket as you are handed your purchases.

However, when studying palms in detail, especially if the lines or markings are quite faint, it can be helpful to accentuate the lines, markings, and even fleshy bumps or mounts on a hand by using talcum powder sprinkled and smoothed on the lines and bumps.

Alternatively, study the hands using a magnifying glass or even a photocopier or a printout of a digital camera photograph of the hand prints. In a hurry, you can draw over the lines and main markings with a marker pen or ballpoint. Paint is a bit messy, though some people do dip their hands in a smooth tray of washable red or blue paint and then go over the hand with a roller before imprinting the hands on paper.

BREAKING THROUGH THE MYSTIQUE

In palmistry, there are no rights and wrongs set in stone and there are many different opinions, so if you intuitively sense a different meaning for a marking or area of a line from what is given in this book or elsewhere, trust yourself.

You will fine-tune your methods through experience, and palmistry is an area where practice really does bring confidence, as you notice certain recurring patterns in different hands, even though—as we know from fingerprinting—each hand is subtly different.

What is more, lines can change within a few months, especially if advice from a previous reading is acted upon, while markings can be gone in weeks or even days, especially those lines and markings that are caused by worry. If a person has masses of small lines in different directions on either hand that don't seem to fit any of the accepted line positions, you can be sure that they are anxiety lines and that the person who has them is worried about a particular issue or has major life stress and may need counseling equally as much as divination.

In time, you will see the relationships in the intersecting, merging, or overlapping of the lines and markings on the lines. Much of the information in the huge formal palmistry books is simply common sense.

The key to successful palm reading is to relax and trust what you feel. The lines and markings serve the same purposes as a tarot card, rune, or crystal; each has a basic meaning, and indeed you may wish to supplement your palmistry with other divinatory methods to confirm, and/or elaborate, on your findings.

The hand is an entry point to the inner soul, to much more than the information offered by these outer markings—though that of course is a vital part of a fully integrated reading. As with any other divinatory form, the questioner is not subject to a fixed fate; but if a subject is directed into one action rather than another, this will be reflected in altered hand lines and markings, albeit subtly in the months and years ahead.

THE DIFFERENCES BETWEEN THE HANDS

As I suggested earlier, the lines on the left or Inactive hand reveal the natural potential self that unfolds during life, our talents, our essential personality, and our thoughts and dreams.

The lines on the right or Active hand reveal the acquired self, formed by circumstance and by people encountered on life's road, present destiny which reflects circumstances and opportunities taken or rejected. The Active hand may also contain elements of the past that are unresolved. If you are older, you will detect these past issues as a break, cross, or grill mark near the beginning or middle of the appropriate line on the dominant hand: for example, where breakups involving children are concerned. What is more, when you pass your fingers over the area, it will feel blocked or dead. I have written a chapter on the all-important markings that are most subject to change.

If a person is left-handed, the right hand will be the hand of potential. The left or potential hand is not static, because our potential is never still, but it unravels at different stages of life. The left hand does not at any single point reflect the entire contents of the individual's book of possibilities, but it reflects merely the menu for the current chapter and the possibilities that are forming just over the horizon. In this way, the Inactive hand is the most predictive, and for this reason should be read either before (my choice) or after the Active hand of current actions and choices. Comparing the two will then bring the whole picture together.

KEEPING A PALMISTRY JOURNAL

A palmistry journal is a good way of recording what you find on your own palms as you work through this book, and as you read for others. Simply mark their unique palm structure on blank diagrams, which you can then draw or stick in the book, along with what you intuitively sense. Use a loose-leaf folder with pages you can add and subdivide, giving regular clients their own section for ongoing sessions.

Initially work with friends and family and yourself, for palmistry is not only an excellent diagnostic tool, but also a good way of monitoring life paths. Younger people, especially teenagers and those in their twenties, quite often will have rapid changes and will benefit from readings about every three months or at major change points.

DEVELOPING YOUR EXPERTISE

Once you are confident of basic meanings, practice as much as you can with as many different subjects: family, young children, older people, those who are in love, teenagers. You will find that once people know that you read palms, colleagues, friends at parties, and anyone who hears you practice the ancient art will approach you with problems. Once you feel confident in your results, an assurance that comes from feedback both during and after readings, you can charge small amounts and, if this feels unnatural—and people do value what they have paid for—then give the money to charity.

If you use the photocopy method or a digital camera (you can get computer programs to convert photos to drawings), then you can stick the images named and dated in your journal and scribble notes on the side.

If you are reading the palms directly, then—as I suggested—either draw the palms in your journal or record the lines on the blank palm diagrams, and attach them. Have lots of blank diagrams ready.

In Chapter 1, we will study the two main and most easily identifiable of the lines on your hand: the line of the Heart and the line of the Head.

LEFT

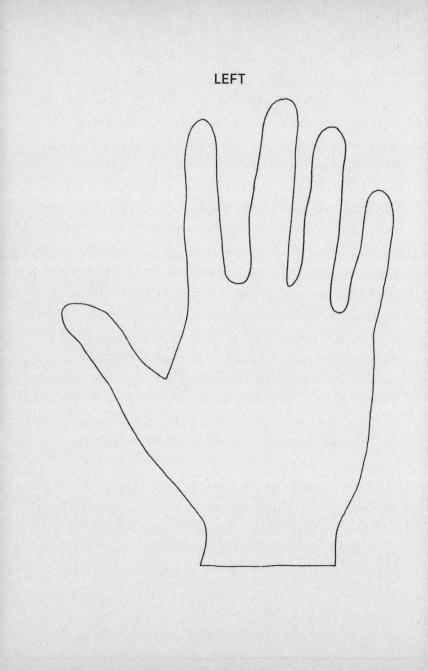

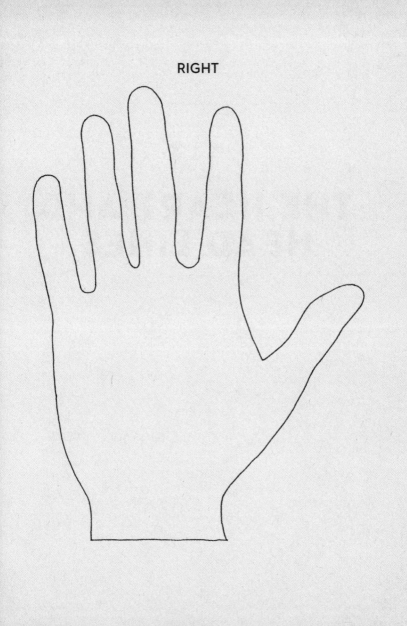

RIGHT

THE HEART AND HEAD LINES

THE AREAS AND LINES OF THE HAND OFFER information on the age-old issues that prompt all divinatory searching: love, success, health, family, money, and happiness.

Two of the most important and easily identifiable lines on the hand—lines that reflect our past, present, and future lives and choices—are the line of the Heart and the line of the Head. You will already have felt the energies of these two lines as you ran your fingers close to these lines, the highest horizontal lines that generally extend across the palms of both hands. You may have sensed blockages or sudden surges of energy at certain points along these lines.

The Heart line, the upper one, is read *left to right across the palm* in the Active hand. The Head line is read *right to left across the palm* in the Active hand. With the Inactive hand, the Heart line is read *right to left* and the Head line is read *left to right* across the palm.

GENERAL INFORMATION ABOUT THE LINES ON THE PALM

All the lines or wrinkles crossing the palms represent pathways that are being, or can be trodden, through life. The mounts—the fleshy mounds around or near the fingers that I have pictured in the diagram below (about which we will learn in a later chapter)—are the repositories of characteristics that can be unfolded in positive or negative ways and can be expressed in the Heart and Head lines. Note whether the Heart or Head line begins in, joins, crosses, or ends at any of the mounts, as these will be of extra influence.

In fact, there are four major lines on the hand. They are the Heart, Head, Life, and Fate or Destiny lines. All four together give a detailed picture of a person's life: the quality, potential, and life choices, the interplay of physical, emotional, intellectual, and spiritual aspects. Ideally all four lines should be clear, well marked, and deep.

If you only learn to read the four major lines—Heart, Head, Life, and Fate or Destiny—that are described in this and the following chapter, you can do very satisfactory palm readings. Indeed, using this and your intuitive method of tuning in to palm energies, you can start to do readings in more detail for others almost at once.

As you are learning the characteristics of the Heart and Head lines, tick or scribble down any that apply to your own lines.

Once you have learned the meanings of the Heart and Head lines, draw your own lines on your individual palm images that you began in the Introduction. As you explore your own Heart and Head lines, observe especially the difference between the lines of your potential on your non-writing hand and the actual development on your dominant hand.

Some palms have only three lines (the Heart, Head, and Life), some only two. The Simian line occurs when the Head and Heart lines form a single line that can result in too much emotion or, conversely, coldness or veering between the two.

Some people have very few lines even on their Active hand (though they may have more on their Inactive hand), just Head and Heart, no branches or significant markings. Such people tend to be very private, not touched by events, don't reveal their feelings, and regard life as black and white.

Generally, the fewer the lines, the easier and less stressful a person's life. However, there may be less incentive for change and action, as often it is the challenges that spur us to change. Most lines are caused by worry, and thus they are relatively transient; in palmistry, the ideal is a balance between very few and very many lines.

Each person is unique, and an apparent weakness in one area can be compensated for in another. On the whole, however, shallow lines in the Active hand tend to indicate a desire to not get too involved in life and love, while any deeper lines indicate a passion for whatever area the specific line refers to.

For example, a deep Head line may indicate a profound love of learning, especially if the Life line is also deep and well formed.

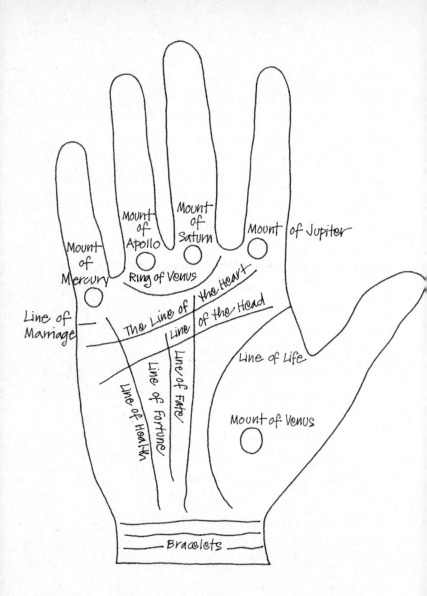

Mount of Apollo

Mount of Saturn

Mount of Jupiter

Mount of Mercury

Ring of Venus

Line of Marriage

The Line of the Heart

Line of the Head

Line of Life

Line of Fate

Line of Fortune

Line of Health

Mount of Venus

Bracelets

THE HEART LINE

Begin by examining your own Heart line with a magnifying glass or another method so that you can tell where it begins on the hand, how it curves, where it ends, how thick and deep it is, and whether there are any significant breaks.

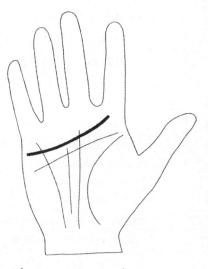

The Heart line, the first to be studied in a reading, reveals information about our emotional state and relationships and anything that is dear to our heart and the potential to grow as a person in every way, what we feel about ourselves, others, and life, with spirit and our inner feelings and the world.

The Heart line often begins around the mount of Mercury at the percussion side of the palm below the little finger above the mount of Luna, running toward the mount of Jupiter, *left to right across the palm on the Active hand,* ending either close to the base of the first two fingers or, most commonly, between them.

It is the highest line to cross the palm below the fingers, with the Head line beneath it. If the Heart line is close to the fingers, it can indicate that emotions may be more restrained than in someone with a lower Heart line. A totally smooth Heart line from beginning to end is rare.

When you learn the meanings of the markings in Chapter 5, you can understand even more of the significance. If you wish, jump ahead if a particular marking intrigues you, or put your index finger over it and feel whether it is positive, a learning experience, or best left behind.

Different Heart Line Formations

- **CLEAR, DEEP, AND LONG LINE:** Emotional depths, being in tune with his or her own feelings, concerned for the needs and problems of others.

- **CURVING AT THE END:** The ability to confidently express innermost needs and feelings.

- **STRAIGHT ACROSS THE PALM, NOT CURVING TOWARD THE FINGERS:** Easily hurt, needing affection and appreciation.

- **COARSE AND GRAINY:** Sensuality or a particularly passionate relationship.

- **PALE, FLAT, AND BROAD:** Sentimentality, but more positively tranquil emotions.

- **CONSISTENTLY BROKEN, OR WITH SEVERAL BRANCHES:** Feelings are initially intense for people, including friendships, but not long-lasting; a tendency to be discouraged when idealism is replaced by reality.

- **CLOSE TO THE BASE OF THE FINGERS, WITH A WIDE SPACE BETWEEN IT AND THE HEAD LINE:** A person unresponsive in relationships and cold in interactions.

- **TOUCHING THE MOUNT OF JUPITER DIRECTLY, OR AS A BRANCH TO IT:** Altruistic and generous in love and any relationship.

- **EXTENDING THROUGH THE JUPITER MOUNT TO THE JUPITER (FIRST) FINGER:** A desire to control relationships and partners; discrimination in choosing partners.

- **ENDING AT THE MOUNT OF SATURN:** Happiness in love; obstacles in relationships are met by determination to find a solution and patience.

- **TOO CLOSE TO THE SATURN (SECOND) FINGER ABOVE THE SATURN MOUNT:** Physical love and outward appearance are significant.

- **TOUCHING THE LIFE LINE:** Oversensitivity, love can become suffocating or possessive.

- **STRAIGHT AND PARALLEL TO THE LIFE LINE:** Emotional stability.

- **FREQUENT LINES CROSSING THE HEART LINE:** Emotional trauma.

- **A LONG, STRAIGHT LINE (ENDING BELOW THE INDEX FINGER):** An awareness of the feelings of others and the ability to empathize with others.

- **UNUSUALLY LONG EDGE TO EDGE OF THE PALM:** Dependency on a partner, family, or close friends.

- **A FAINT LINE:** Being dominated or bullied or with a very delicate energy field.

- **SHORT, STRAIGHT LINE (ENDING BETWEEN THE MIDDLE AND INDEX FINGERS):** Unromantic, demonstrating love through actions, not words.

- **A LONG, CURVED LINE (ARCHING TO REACH THE BASE OF THE MIDDLE FINGER):** Tendency to follow desires, romantic impulses, and passions.

- **A LINE SPLIT IN TWO:** Putting the needs of others first.

- **SIMILARITY TO A PARTNER'S:** This indicates compatibility.

- **SPLITTING INTO THREE TO FORM A TRIDENT:** Luck in love and life.

- **ENDING BETWEEN FIRST AND SECOND FINGERS:** Balance in relationships.

- **A PRONOUNCED GIRDLE OF VENUS (SEE DIAGRAM IN THIS CHAPTER AND CHAPTER 4), RELATED CLOSELY TO THE HEART LINE:** A need for physical intimacy and, if deep, great sensuality.

- **A CONSISTENTLY CHAINED LINE:** Maybe more than one love relationship going on at the same time, conflicting emotions, and sometimes past life/karmic unfinished business.

THE HEAD LINE

This is the line running across the palm from the side of the hand between the thumb and the forefinger to the mount of the Moon area of the hand or above toward the little finger side, *right to left in the Active Hand, below the Heart line*. Its links with other mounts and lines are especially influential, and it is the second line to be studied in a palm reading.

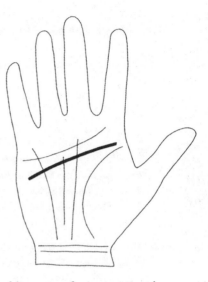

Remember, the Heart and Head lines start from opposite sides of the hand. The Head line can have several starting points, for example from the Life line, whose energies thereby reinforce natural determination in the Head line. Another beginning is at the mount of Jupiter, which can indicate great authority and wisdom—but, on the negative side, egoism.

The Head line expresses how our thoughts and intellect are manifest in our lives; our logic and rational dealings with the world and those around us; and what we think, as opposed to what we feel about ourselves, our outer persona as revealed to the world. Look especially at any parallels between the Heart and Head lines: for example, if one fades or is crossed with lines as the other becomes strong.

Different Head Line Formations

If the Heart and Head lines are very close, there can be a conflict between the Heart and Head. If the Heart line is joined to the Head line, relationships may suffer because of work or outside interests being a priority.

- **IF THE HEAD LINE TOUCHES THE LIFE LINE AT THE START:** Indicates a cautious person who thinks before s/he acts. When there is a gap between the start of the Head line and Life line, the person will be independent and impulsive; and the larger the gap, the more outspoken, impulsive, and independent s/he will be.

- **IF THE LINE IS HIGH AND IT DOES NOT BEGIN OR MEET WITH THE LIFE LINE:** Independence from birth, own ideas, may be a rift between person and immediate family; the person is happier with facts and figures than people.

- **IF THE LINE IS CLOSE TO THE THUMB OR JOINS THE LIFE LINE FOR A LENGTH:** A cautious, conservative thinker and a family-minded person who may have a family-based or home business.

- **BEGINNING BELOW THE LIFE LINE:** Shyness from childhood, perhaps an absent parent, over-defensiveness at work and socially due to hidden insecurity.

- **A LONG, WELL-FORMED LINE:** Justice and idealism.

- **A LONG LINE ARCHING SLIGHTLY TOWARD MOUNT LUNA WITHOUT DIPPING DOWN SUDDENLY:** Many interests and an openness to learning.

- **A WAVY HEAD LINE:** Influenced by different people and finding it hard to make decisions.

- **A DEEP LINE:** Concentration and memorization will be easy.

- **A STRONGLY MARKED LINE:** Intelligence and imagination, logic and determination, but, less positively, also a touch of ruthlessness.

- **A SHORT LINE (ENDING NEAR THE CENTER OF THE PALM):** A fast thinker and with unlimited capacity to learn, but can be impatient with traditional learning.

- **A PALE, SHORT LINE:** Timidity and diffidence in career or social dealings.

- **A FAINT LINE:** Intellectual and reasoning ability is not being fully used.

- **A STRAIGHT LINE:** A logical, practical down-to-earth approach and, if extending to the little finger, a tendency toward analyzing every situation and sometimes over-thinking.

- **LINE CURVING TOWARD THE WRIST:** A creative, imaginative approach to life, good at finding alternative solutions.

- **A REALLY LARGE CURVE:** Gifts in creative arts (check with the Apollo Sun line in Chapter 4), but also liberal with the truth.

- **A FORK AT THE END OF THE HEAD LINE:** The Writer's fork, the mark of the writer and communicator.

- **AN UPWARD BRANCH ANYWHERE ON THE LINE:** Skills in making money and a good gambler.

- **A BRANCH CONNECTING THE HEAD AND HEART LINES:** Confusion if emotions override common sense.

- **A DISTINCTIVE BEND AT THE END:** Strong material needs.

- **A SPLIT LINE:** The ability to see both sides of a question—or sit on the fence.

- **BROKEN LINES:** Many options that have not been followed through; changes should not be made out of restlessness or boredom.

- **STARTING ON MOUNT JUPITER:** Influenced by ambitions; if well developed, a good teacher or instructor.

- **CONTINUING IN A STRAIGHT LINE RIGHT ACROSS THE PALM:** A practical approach, good business sense and persistence.

- **DIPPING DEEPLY TOWARD THE MOUNT OF THE MOON:** Overindulgence; and if the mount is well developed, sign of a dreamer.

- **A DOUBLE HEAD LINE:** Either genius or double-dealing, sometimes both.

Timing

There are many conflicting opinions about timing events on the Active hand, and the simplest method is to divide the Head and Heart lines in two. The first half of the Head line on the Active hand starts from the edge of the hand and ends under the Saturn finger, and represents ages 0 to 40. The second half shows 40 to the end of life, which is never defined.

Alternatively, you can use the Fate or Destiny line if this is clearly marked on the active palm. By age 35, the Fate or Destiny line reaches the Head line. By 49, the Destiny line reaches the Heart line, and the rest marks out the remainder of life. The length of life is not indicated by any line or measurement, and I do not believe that any clairvoyant or medium can know this date of death, for themselves or others—or indeed should. Many heartaches are caused by irresponsible people predicting the deaths of others to satisfy their own egos.

Remember, though, if matters are resolved and an event was some years ago, it may at least have been partly erased; so if you are trying to predict the future, the most useful function of palmistry, look when new lines either of independence or new love become smooth and deep—and may indeed form parallel or overlapping lines.

WORKING WITH THE HEART AND HEAD LINES

Once you have plotted your own lines on your blank diagram, try to study at least ten other people's Heart and Head lines; people you do not know very well, perhaps in the workplace or socially, and if possible try to make some contact with the palm, so you can add what you feel.

This is not as hard as it may at first seem. If you are ingenious, there will be many occasions when someone will have at least one of their palms in full view for a minute or two.

If you can see both hands, so much the better. Scribble it down and later copy the information on a blank sheet. Then with the lists above, check what characteristics you found. If you can ask casual questions, you can determine how accurate your observations are. But remember, people won't always tell the truth about their lives.

Next, study the Heart and then the Head line of the person whose hands you held and felt in detail in the Introduction, and compare the new information that you can add to the original palm diagrams and your intuitive reading.

Practice drawing some of the Heart/Head combinations from the above list and create imaginary people based on the Heart and Head lines. Be alert to Heart and Head line combinations everywhere, even fleeting glances of the hands of people you encounter at social events, traveling, or in your working day. You will soon see patterns emerging and be able to make fast assessments of hands.

THE HEART AND HEAD LINES AND TEENAGERS

You may find in teenagers quite wavy Heart Lines with frequent breaks as teenage romances ebb and flow. Head Lines may, sometimes in correspondingly similar areas, have lots of stops and starts and varying thickness and intensity, as career choices and enthusiasms wax and wane. Let's take, for example, sixteen-year old Cleo. For about nine months, Cleo consistently revealed a pulsating deep and intense Heart Line because love was her current main interest. However, her Head line became correspondingly relatively pale approximately nine months ago as her early career dreams took second place to romance. Her previous boyfriend, with whom she broke up three months ago, had a very deep straight Head Line, but a wavy paler Heart Line, as he was intensely driven by his parents to give up Cleo and focus on career.

In contrast, Cleo's new boyfriend's Heart Line mirrors hers, and even within six months of getting together their corresponding Head Lines are getting similarly stronger as they plan to go to college together next year.

In the next chapter, we will study the Life line and the Fate or Destiny line.

2

THE LINES OF LIFE AND FATE OR DESTINY

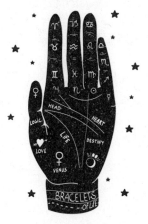

ONCE YOU HAVE LEARNED THE LIFE LINE AND the Fate or Destiny line, you can do good readings, combined with the intuitive method of assessing what you have learned. The ultimate aim of palmistry is to answer people's questions about their lives, and so it is important to see both in the Inactive hand and the Active Hand the strengths and potentials to fulfill dreams and overcome obstacles. For every pitfall or weakness you identify on a line and other areas of the palm in future readings, match it with a strength revealed in the lines and other parts of the palm to suggest a good way forward. Palmistry by its intimate nature should be a two-way ongoing dialogue so the subject can see for themselves as you interpret on the hand map how the past and present can be used to draw on talents and strengths still in reserve.

ABOUT THE LIFE LINE AND THE FATE OR DESTINY LINE

The line of Life mirrors the life force coursing through us. It does not reveal how long we will live, whatever its length, but speaks of our passion for life, our pleasure in living, and physical energy. Where there are breaks or pale areas, it is a good indicator if someone is lacking enthusiasm or energy and not maximizing the potentials of the Heart and Head lines.

The Fate or Destiny line shows whether you control your own destiny; and by studying it, you may decide to take charge of your future if others are too influential. The Fate or Destiny line also expresses the sense of purpose about life and how important it is to an individual to become successful or take a more *laissez-faire* approach.

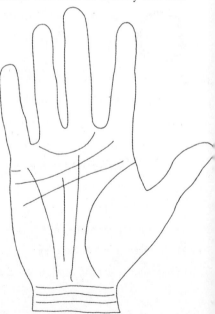

The following diagram will help you to identify the lines of Life and Fate or Destiny, in relation to the other major lines on the palm.

Once you have discovered these two lines on your

own hand, you can mark them on your evolving personal hand diagrams and see how the four main lines interact: which is the strongest and clearest, and which is the weakest. Don't worry if your Fate line is not clear or indeed starts halfway up the hand, as this and the other vertically running lines can be less obvious initially. But with practice you will spot them.

THE LIFE LINE

This runs in a curve from above the thumb, between the thumb and the forefinger, to below the thumb, ending on or near the wrist, sweeping in a semicircle around the thumb.

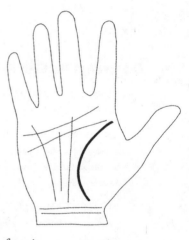

The more impetus put into life, the stronger and deeper the Life line will be, not only physically, but in the pulsating positive vibrations that can be sensed, if you run your hand over the line to feel the vibrations emanating from it.

The amount of palm it encircles is important. A Life line well across the palm reveals a great deal of stamina and energy, an adventurous person, taking chances, making the most of any opportunity. If the Life line hugs the thumb, the person may be listless and unenthusiastic and may need to rebalance priorities. Ultimately it reveals how enthusiastic and passionate a person is for life and the degree of pleasure they derive from that life. Short, pale Life lines usually lengthen and deepen as life goes on if the possessor finds his/her true destiny that excites and stimulates.

The Life line is especially prone to the effects of stress, and we know that if someone has a delicate energy field, toxic people and situations may cause crosses or grilles and other negative marks (see Chapter 5) to temporarily appear. Overcome the problem, and this can sometimes involve letting go of past unfairness, and they will disappear.

Different Life Line Formations

- **LONG AND WELL DEFINED LINE WITH A BROAD CURVE:** An achiever, but not ruthless in life.

- **UNBROKEN AND SMOOTH:** A potentially smooth passage through life, which may be less exciting than a line with many breaks and chains. Sometimes challenges or setbacks can act as a spur for success.

- **STRAIGHT AND CLOSE TO THE EDGE OF THE HAND:** Caution in relationships and in accepting life challenges or the unfamiliar.

- **STARTING CLOSE TO THE FIRST (JUPITER) FINGER:** Drive to fulfill ambitions.

- **STARTING CLOSER TO THE THUMB:** An easygoing approach to life.

- **CONTINUING CLOSE TO THE THUMB:** Prone to tiredness/inertia under stress.

- **DIPPING/CURVING SHARPLY TO THE BASE OF THE PALM:** An opportunity/incentive to take a new direction that may seem difficult, but may ultimately prove worthwhile.

- **BREAKS GENERALLY:** Changes in outlook on life; how they are handled determines success.

- **BREAKS IN THE UPWARD DIRECTION TOWARD THE EDGE OF THE HAND:** An imminent journey of positive significance, even if not planned at the time of the reading.

- **FINE SMALL SISTER LINE ON THUMB SIDE:** Good fortune; if extends the whole length of line, good health in later life.

- **DEEP:** Strong feelings, leaping into life and embracing every experience.

- **RED OR BROWN:** Demonstrative and passionate.

- **LACKING COLOR:** Does not share experiences and feelings with others.

- **SHORT AND SHALLOW:** Easily manipulated or conned.

- **CHAINED THROUGHOUT:** Many options and choices in life.

- **FORKS:** Scattered and sometimes wasted energies.

- **DOUBLE:** Soulmate love present or coming.

- **VERY SHORT, JOINING THE LINE OF FATE:** Momentous changes caused by external events, that if handled positively can offer exciting opportunities.

- **BRANCHES OR EFFORT LINES, ACCORDING TO THE MOUNT, FINGER, OR OTHER LINE THEY JOIN:** Indicate a surge toward money, success, or love (Chapters 5 and 6).

THE FATE OR DESTINY LINE

The Fate or Destiny line, sometimes called the line of Saturn, in its ideal fully developed form runs vertically up the middle of the hand, from midway between the mount of the Moon and the mount of Venus toward the second finger of Saturn. Not everyone has a Fate or Destiny line, and in fact it can start anywhere near the base of the hand and finish close to any finger. However, most Fate lines in practice start close to or touching the Life line and head toward the second finger.

This line is often faint and refers to what is called the interplay of Luck or Fate in one's life. Its full development or clarity does not necessarily indicate good luck, but a tendency to a reaction to life's unexpected challenges, both good and bad, in fulfilling life's purpose, rather than leaving results to Fate or others. It is the vehicle through which the potential of the Heart, Head, and Life lines manifest themselves.

However, it is also relatively common to have an arched or curved Fate line. Neither is better. A straight Fate or Destiny line can indicate a more focused life plan and path, whereas a wavering Fate line could indicate the path of someone who spends time exploring or searching for the best-fitting life purpose to undertake—and it can become straighter as the definite choices are made.

It can be fused to other lines, especially the Apollo or Fortune line that rises to the third Apollo or Sun finger to the left in the Active hand, and one line can form a branch of the other.

At its clearest and longest, the Fate or Destiny line extends from the base of the hand to the finger of Saturn, and indicates (not as traditionally thought: that Fate will always favor the possessor) that the suggested pathway will be successful—because of the immense resources of the possessor—to change difficulty into challenge and to adapt rather than be defeated by outside events.

Some Fate lines do not appear until a person is in their 20s or 30s. Since it is estimated that the Fate line crosses the Head line at about age 35, some Fate lines naturally begin on or near the Head line in the 30s or even 40s when career and life paths are more settled. However, when a child knows from an early age or is directed by parents into an education and a career traditionally followed by family members, such as the military, teaching, or law, the Fate line will appear clearly and straight near the base of the palm from early on in life and rise to the second Saturn finger.

Different Fate Line Formations

- **DEEP AND PROMINENT: Controlled by Destiny and what life offers.**

- **JOINED TO LIFE LINE: Making your own future.**

- **STARTING AT THE BASE OF THE PALM AND EXTENDING UPWARD TO THE JUPITER MOUNT OR FINGER: The ability to gain public recognition or follow a career path pre-ordained from childhood or past worlds.**

- **VERY PALE AND WAVY OR DISAPPEARING IN PLACES:** Uncertainty, overly influenced by others, and a tendency to be easily discouraged, but often dramatically improves once this characteristic is acknowledged.

- **BROKEN:** Career interruption or loss of motivation; if the line continues in a different place, new career path.

- **BROKEN BUT OVERLAPPING:** Development of hobby or interest into predominant career, following dreams.

- **CENTRALLY EVOLVING, WITH BREAKS AND MARKINGS, FROM MIDDLE OF PALM:** Obstacles early on in life that have served or will serve to change and determine the life course for the better.

- **LINKS WITH THE LIFE LINE:** Determination in meeting challenges and a breadth of perspective that can enable problems to be avoided.

- **IF LINK IS LONG WITH LIFE LINE:** Close to family but may feel undue obligations/guilt.

- **IF AWAY FROM LIFE LINE, HALFWAY OR MORE ACROSS PALM:** Independence from early on from family and other authority influences.

- **ABSENT:** Very strong karmic/past life influences, need to determine own course in present life rather than repeating old patterns.

- **FAINT:** Feeling at the mercy of Fate, drifting through life, unsettled career path. If it disappears, may be due to bullying, undue pressure.

- **FORKED:** Two alternative destinies according to choices made/to be made.

- **EXCEPTIONALLY STRONG, CLEAR, UNWAVERING FROM START TO FINISH:** Competitive in any career or sport, striving and achieving the best, whatever it takes.

- **BEGINNING ON MOUNT OF VENUS:** Motivations strongly influenced by family, good at physical activity.

- **BEGINNING ON MOUNT OF MOON:** Self-motivator, follows dreams.

- **ENDING ON HEART LINE:** May give up career ascent for love or have other priorities, such as life quality; may retire early or take up fulfilling rather than lucrative lifestyle.

- **ENDING ON HEAD LINE:** Set in career/lifestyle by middle age; if exceptionally pale, may indicate burnout.

- **ENDING UNDER FIRST INDEX JUPITER FINGER FROM ANY POSITION:** Gifted in politics, religion, law, teaching, benevolent leadership; can rise high.

- **ENDING UNDER SECOND SATURN FINGER OR BETWEEN SECOND AND THIRD FINGERS:** Will do well in any chosen career path, especially conventional salaried appointments.

- **EXTENDING RIGHT UP INTO SECOND SATURN FINGER:** Exceptional destiny, may succeed in psychic work and/or materially.

- **ENDING UNDER THIRD SUN/APOLLO FINGER:** Creative arts, design, imagination often manifest in writing.

- **DIAGONALLY CROSSING PALM TO LITTLE/MERCURY FINGER:** Communicator, business success, salesperson, entertainer, medicine, money-making abilities.

- **DOUBLE DESTINY LINE FOR ANY PART:** Versatility or may follow two careers or career and important hobby that eventually becomes second career or combine career/family.

Timings for Life and Fate

There are many alternative ways of calculating timings on all four lines. Decide or adapt a method that works in practice for you, or simply use your intuition over timings. It may be that the same system works for you on all four lines. The real key is looking at change points in the line markings that may reveal sticking points from the past.

The Life line traditionally divides from the beginning of the line in increments of ten to the end 80/90 plus. You can in practice use this method for Heart, Head, and Fate or Destiny as well, as it is relatively straightforward.

Another method divides the Life line initially into two, the first half nearest the wrist representing the first 20 years of life, and the other half divided into two again. The first part of the divided second half signifies 20 to 50, and the rest of the Life line is the remainder of the person's life.

A traditional method of measuring the Fate line is to divide the distance between the bottom crease of the second Saturn finger to the wrist line into four equal parts. The first quarter begins from the wrist line and deals with the first 21 years, the second represents 22 to 29 years of age, the third 30 to 50 years, and the final 50 to 100 years. This however, only works with a clear long Fate line starting on the wrist, which many don't. If the Fate line does begin higher on the hand, imagine the line extending from the wrist upward and divide as above.

Balancing the Lines

The lines are closely linked with one another, and now you can consider the interconnections like a growing jigsaw puzzle. A predominant Heart line indicates emotions as the driving force and, if the Head line is not sufficiently strong to harness these emotions, then these creative energies may not be channeled into worldly success but may, however, be used for a fulfilling love and family life or to develop a passionate interest. Equally, if the Head line is strong but the Life line is weak, there may not be enough drive to carry through plans and so there may have been a series of half-finished projects or careers that did not flourish.

The relative strengths may change at different times of life and can suggest where other aspects need to come to the fore. It can be especially helpful to compare the four major lines in both hands so that potential and undeveloped strengths can be utilized to create a balanced life.

USING PALMISTRY FOR POSITIVE CHANGE

As in Chapter 1 with the Heart and Head lines, once you have added and analyzed your Life and Fate or Destiny lines to your own hand diagrams, study the hands of the person whom you have been following closely and see how the lines build up the picture of the person you know.

Study also the Life and Fate lines of people you meet in different careers, different ages, and different lifestyles—you will by now be getting good at quick assessment. Using the descriptions of different line formations in this chapter, see how the outer appearance, career, and lifestyle of the person coincide with the line markings. Where possible, gently question people whose hands you study.

But palmistry is more than a diagnostic tool; it's primarily an instrument for positive change.

When you feel ready, work with someone with whom you feel comfortable and ask them if they have any questions.

Feel by running your fingers over each major line on the Active hand from beginning to end, to identify where the past still is having a negative effect. Relax, and you may see images in your mind and impressions of the issues, and then tactfully ask questions.

USING PALMISTRY CREATIVELY

When I read the palm of 50-year-old James, who was frustrated in his career and felt he had never achieved anything, he had a broken Head line occurring early on. This felt heavy and slow. It did not pick up in clarity or depth in the ensuing Head line. The break coincided with a serious setback at school when his bullying teachers and father told him that he was useless and would never achieve anything because, although he was intelligent, he had trouble reading and writing. In his case, the Fate line started much higher on the Heart line and ended on the creative Apollo mount of the third finger. I asked about his creative passions and how developing these could offer him fulfillment. Many an artist or writer deterred at school or by parents will flourish, given the activation of the passion of the Heart line or even an intersection of Life-line energy with the dormant Head line. James went for tests and discovered that he had undiagnosed dyslexia; with the help of a good spell-checker and some extra night classes, he is now moving toward his dream of becoming a writer.

Always remember, the point is to be of help in enabling another person to fulfill their destiny in their own way, not to prove how good you are.

In the next chapter, we will work with other subsidiary but very relevant lines on the palm.

3

THE SUBSIDIARY LINES AND OTHER MAJOR AREAS OF THE PALM

YOU CAN DO GOOD READINGS JUST BASED ON the four major lines. However, by considering subsidiary lines as well, the greater detail you get from that enriches your reading and enables you to advise clients how potential weaknesses and pitfalls in one area of the palm—and so in life itself—can be compensated for by drawing on the strengths of other energy sources. For these minor lines, use a magnifying glass. Since the following three lines are not so clear, focus on the Fate line and see if there are others following the vertical path up the palm in the suggested positions. But don't worry if you are having difficulty doing this, as the same qualities are found in other areas of the hand.

THE APOLLO OR SUN LINE, THE FORTUNE LINE

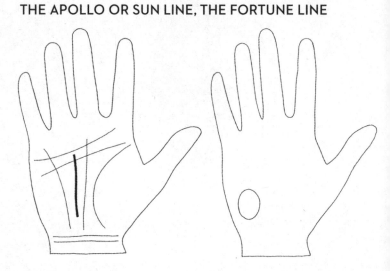

The most important subsidiary line, the Apollo line, begins around the mount of the Moon and usually starts close to the Head line and runs up to the third finger, the Apollo finger or Mount of Apollo, which is often referred to as the ring finger. It runs parallel to the Fate or Destiny line for part of its length. It is similar to and often confused with the line of Fate. Some people will have only one of these lines; some others have both, but they join.

The Apollo line represents worldly success in both monetary terms and achievements. It is often short, compared with the major lines.

People who have an Apollo line are confident socially, with great potential for success.

- **STARTING PART OF THE WAY UP THE PALM:** Indicates its appearance at the time a person decides on their goal and goes all-out.

- **STARTING NEARER THE PALM (RARER):** Seen in those who want to be musicians, writers, or athletes from childhood, often accompanied by a long clear Fate line.

- **DEEP AND CLEAR:** Indicates good fortune, often recognition or even fame accompanied by material rewards, usually linked with the arts; the more pronounced, the greater the fame and fortune. Also can indicate acquired wealth through luck or inheritance rather than hard work.

- **ABSENT:** Can be compensated for by a well-formed Apollo mount and finger, as often the person who strives achieves more than one who has it all.

THE HEALTH LINE OR THE LINE OF MERCURY OR HEPATICA B

This crosses the center of the hand, ending close to the Heart line or the mount of Mercury, close to the little Mercury finger, running diagonally across the palm from close to or inside the Life line near to the wrist. It refers to physical health, although it is also connected to mental and spiritual well-being.

The Health line is nowhere near as clear as the other lines crossing the palm and may be confused with a branch from the Fate line, especially if the Fate line is not in its usual position in the middle of the hand.

- **IF ABSENT:** Not a bad omen, rather indicates that there's nothing to worry about and you recover quickly from illness.

- **IF CLEAR AND WELL MARKED:** Excellent health; often may appear after you have recovered from a major emotional or physical setback.

- **WAVY, BADLY FORMED, OR PALE:** Check your diet and lifestyle, as it indicates not the onset of illness but that maybe you need to take better care of yourself. This can be the sign of a very sensitive individual, who reacts badly to toxic people or negative environments and so maybe a change of career or lifestyle is all that is needed to maintain health and for this line to firm up.

THE INTUITION LINE

This line, also known as the line of the psychic self, extends in a curve from the center of the Mount of the Moon, passing through the Head and Heart lines almost to the marriage/relationship lines, the horizontal lines below the Mercury little finger on the percussion of the Hand (see

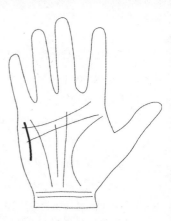

the main diagram in Chapter 1 for the exact position of the marriage lines). It represents at its clearest a well-developed intuitive sense or evolved psychic abilities. Again, a line easily mistaken.

- **WELL DEVELOPED, ESPECIALLY LEADING TOWARD THE FATE LINE:** A medium or clairvoyant.

- **LEADING TOWARD THE HEAD LINE:** A natural healer.

THE RING OF SOLOMON OR JUPITER

This is a semicircular ring marking and so unmistakable, but not always present, circling the base of the Jupiter finger and sometimes surrounding the Mount of Jupiter. It indicates an interest in the psychic, in ancient wisdom, an ability for precognitive dreams, intuitive awareness mixed with wisdom and strong altruistic desires, and fascination with psychology.

GIRDLE OR RING OF VENUS

This often blends in with part of the Heart line, running from the space between the Jupiter and Saturn fingers to the space between the Saturn and Apollo fingers or between the Apollo and Mercury fingers, similar to a crescent moon hanging over the Heart line.

The Girdle of Venus indicates the need to create emotional boundaries to avoid swings of emotion and compensatory over-indulgence to absorb suppressed hurt.

- **MADE UP OF SEVERAL THIN LINES:** A very sensitive nature.

- **CONNECTED TO THE HEART LINE:** A very tender, devoted, but sometimes oversensitive lover.

- **CLEAR AND WELL FORMED:** Loves beauty, sensual nature.

- **BROKEN:** Charming, amorous but can be unfaithful.

- **STRAIGHT, CLOSE TO THE HEART LINE:** Good with money and lucky with it.

THE LINE OF MARS

This runs parallel to the Life line on the thumb side line, not found on every hand. It gives support and strength to the Life line and enables a person to deal effectively and nonaggressively with conflict.

THE LINE OF MONEY

This is an upright line under the ring and little fingers.

- **DEEP, CLEAR, STRAIGHT: Many good opportunities for making money, good for investments, speculation.**

- **IF A BRANCH (CALLED A MONEY LINE ALSO) FROM APOLLO LINE JOINS THE MONEY LINE: Good for commercial success, business ventures.**

- **IF APOLLO LINE ALSO STRAIGHT AND CLEAR: Great wealth.**

- **WAVY LINES: Wealth will be unstable, tendency to lose it or give it away.**

TRAVEL LINES

Travel lines are fine lines that can be both vertical and horizontal, starting vertically from the edge of the palm at the base and coming up toward the mount of the Moon on the little finger Mercury side of the hand and opposite the thumb, or horizontally and slightly diagonally from the edge of the wrist at the bottom of the Life line. Both types, especially the vertical, may intersect, be near, or travel through the Life line.

- **STRONG AND NUMEROUS TRAVEL LINES:** Restlessness that can lead to frequent travel.

- **CLEARLY FORMED:** Opportunities and incentive to travel or to live, work, or study or emigrate overseas.

- **DEEP HORIZONTAL LINES, FORMED FROM OR EMERGING FROM THE LIFE LINE:** Opportunities and good fortune in making a living overseas.

- **A HORIZONTAL LINE JOINING THE FATE LINE AND CURVING DOWN TO THE MOUNT OF THE MOON:** Profitable overseas travel and, if either kind of line intersects with the Fate line, positive life-changing travel. Maybe marrying overseas.

- **ABSENT OR SHORT:** Little desire to travel far. Check the Inactive hand to see if there are travel lines that have not been manifested because of circumstances or perhaps a bad experience traveling, or if the possessor is naturally a homebody and so should not feel pressured to travel.

VIA LASCIVIA

This is a straight line that runs part of the way across the palm starting two thirds to three quarters of the way down the palm from the mount of the Moon on the Mercury finger side; may stop on the Moon mount or reach the mount of Venus under the thumb. People possessing this line constantly need stimulation and may not know when to stop.

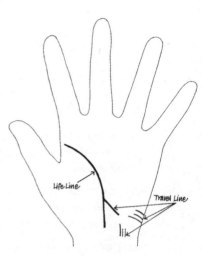

- **VERY STRONG:** An addictive personality; but if this power is harnessed, it can lead to the fulfilment of a powerful dream or desire.

MARRIAGE/RELATIONSHIP LINES

(See Chapters 1 and 2 for diagrams showing the Marriage/Relationship lines.)
These are fine lines that extend slightly diagonally across the side of the palm between the start of the Heart line and the Mercury finger. They refer to any serious relationships that may or may not be sexual. Though there may be several parallel lines, if a person is very loving but in a settled relationship from a relatively young age, any other lines will be manifested as close friendships or deep family connections, perhaps with a sibling, a mentor, or a close parental link. A lifetime love tends only to manifest as one.

Look at the longest line as the key or current one; and if you are in an unhappy relationship, you may see another waiting above.

- **CLEAR, WELL MARKED, COMING FROM THE SIDE OF THE HAND AND ONTO THE SURFACE OF THE PALM:** A major relationship.

- **TOUCHING THE APOLLO/SUN LINE:** A new career success as a result of, or after, getting married; successful business and love combined.

- **ABSENT LINES:** Lack of emotional commitment even if married or an independent person who will always want independence, even when in a committed relationship.

- **BROKEN LINE:** An unresolved love that may stop other relationships from growing.

- **SHORT LINE, HARDLY REACHING THE PALM SURFACE:** The relationship may need hard work, or a decision needs to be made as to whether the relationship is really worth it.

Note: a line can disappear if there is a major breakup, but a new line may appear when a new relationship appears, or when the possessor is ready for new love.

CHILDREN LINES

Fine vertical lines immediately below the Mercury finger, sometimes overlapping the marriage/relationship lines. These show a woman's potential to have children; but in the modern age, this is of course dependent upon the choice of the parents, and some will choose to use this potential affinity with children to care for children in teaching, social care, fostering, or with nieces and nephews. Equally, it does not predict whether the babies will be conceived naturally or with medical help. Traditionally, it is said that longer lines indicate boys and shorter lines, girls.

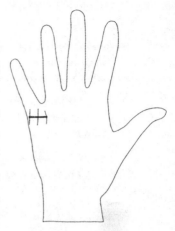

For a man, children lines indicate that a man will be a good father/have good relations professionally or with stepchildren.

RASCETTES, BRACELET LINES ON THE INNER WRIST IMMEDIATELY BELOW THE PALM
(See Chapters 1 and 2 main diagrams for Rascettes position.)
Romanies traditionally claim that each bracelet represents 25 years of life, and people can have up to four, but usually three or four. There is no truth whatsoever in the old belief that a first (top) broken line indicates gynecological problems—this is mere superstition.

Bracelet 1: Refers to Health and is Closest to the Palm
- **IF CLEAR, UNBROKEN:** A robust constitution, resistant to illness and stress.

- **IF BROKEN:** A lack of care of own health (often those who care for others rather than themselves); a sign to focus on healthy eating, gentle exercise, and reducing stress; also those who had to work hard in early life to overcome obstacles.

Bracelet 2: Refers to Prosperity

- **IF UNBROKEN:** Financial and life success, often follows efforts expressed in first rascette.

- **IF A TRIANGLE ON IT:** Financial opportunities from many directions; more than one triangle, a successful new business venture.

- **BROKEN:** More of a struggle and setbacks financially that have longer-term effects but can be overcome.

Bracelets 3 and 4: Refer to Authority and Status

- **IF CLEARLY DEFINED:** Influence in community and officially.

- **IF BROKEN:** May prefer own company or close family.

- **IF THERE IS ONLY ONE BRACELET:** Feel intuitively what it is saying about one or all three issues.

- **IF THERE ARE NO BRACELETS:** You may be giving too much to others in terms of time, money, and not taking credit for your strengths.

WORKING WITH THE NEW INFORMATION

First look on both hands, using a magnifying glass, and identify those lines that you can easily spot. Mark them on your diagrams that now are getting quite full, and spend a bit of time looking at the web of lines, and see how the two hands compare and what potential waits for you to develop. If in doubt, focus on the four main lines and the three subsidiaries until you feel more confident.

Have a look at the hands of the person you have been working closely with too, but don't expect to find all the lines in this chapter.

The main tool in palm reading, as well as intuition, is common sense. You aren't going to remember all the meanings or line positions until you have been doing palmistry for years, though with practice you will soon see recurring patterns in different hands. But if a line is short, wavy, or broken, or is pale and shallow, then clearly there are issues connected with the line (check back with this chapter for its name). Even so, if one is strong and clear, it is functioning well unless it seems too dominant. Curvy is flowing, straight means a direct energy.

STRENGTHENING YOUR ENERGIES AND ENERGIES THROUGH YOUR PALMS

The palm has powerful chakras or energy centers, one in each finger and the thumb, a major one on the heel of the wrist, and another major one in the center of each palm.

You have felt their energies as you ran your hand close to the opposite palm. As well as being a diagnostic tool and a powerful form of divination, at its most creative, palm reading offers the chance to free extra powers for life and happiness through working with the palms, by releasing some of the resources dormant especially in the Inactive hand that expresses the untapped resources within our whole energy system. Palms are also a powerful and easy entry point for empowering yourself, as the energies will flow through your palms to fill your system with well-being, and these new energies will be marked as strengthening palm lines in the weeks and months to come. The Active hand transmits energy, and the Inactive potential hand receives it.

Once a week, put your hands together vertically and press the palms gently but firmly for a minute or two to transfer needed resources from the hand of potential to the Active hand, and to put the hands in balance by passing any excess energies in the Active hand to wait in the potential until called. This is even more effective if you stand on grass barefoot and rotate your hands from side to side as you press them together.

Crystal Palm Power

Buy a palm or worry stone. This is a large flat oval smooth crystal with a central indentation for the thumb. Many palm stones are opaque, and some are richly patterned, made from balancing agate or strengthening jasper. A gentle purple amethyst palm stone will restore all into harmony and heal any imbalances via your palms into your whole energy system. Rose quartz helps strengthen the Heart line, citrine the Head line, clear quartz the Life line, and turquoise the line of Fate.

Initially, hold it between your hands while you do the above exercise and then gently place your thumb in the indentation holding the stone, first in your Inactive hand and then in your Active hand, each for a minute or two. Held between the thumb and forefinger, the palm stone if gently rubbed over the palm dramatically reduces stress levels and releases natural endorphins.

Finally, massage the stone gently over the lines, giving extra time to any that are weak, shallow, or wavy, first holding it in your Active hand to massage the Inactive hand, then changing hands.

Wash the stone under running water after use.

In the next chapter, we will study the mounts that act as repositories of power.

✧ 4 ✧

THE MOUNTS

THERE ARE SEVEN MAIN FLESHY CONTOURS THAT appear on the palm of the hand. Some are named after their ruling finger, but all have planetary names to indicate their significance, and also so astrology can be a good sister art to palmistry.

The mounts act as repositories of power and energy for those areas of the hand they dominate, and also for the fingers that have corresponding planetary names and meanings.

In general, the larger and more pronounced a mount, the stronger the characteristic in the person. Every chance you get, look at the mounts on people's hands and you will soon have an idea of what an average-sized mount looks like.

Use a magnifying glass to identify your own mounts, while holding your hand at eye level, and you may notice that one or more is especially developed. The firmness can be assessed by gently

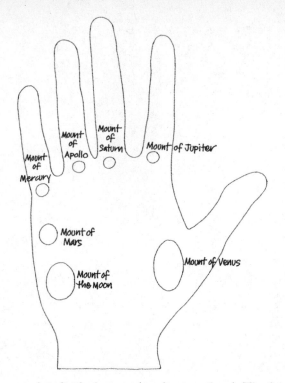

pressing on each individual mount (see diagram above). The firmer the mount, the more its talents are being expressed in one's everyday life. If all mounts seem absent, the possessor may have lacked opportunities or faced discouragement in life. Look for strengths in other parts of the hand, and always emphasize more positive than negative factors. In this way, the subject can see how a weakness is a challenge to be overcome using untapped strengths, especially on the Inactive hand, not a doom-or-gloom-forever prediction.

It may be that the mounts are more pronounced on the potential Inactive hand, but the Active hand mounts can be strengthened by the techniques I suggested in the previous chapter and the pendulum healing method I describe later in this chapter. Practice is the key to assessing the relative sizes and fleshiness or otherwise of mounts, so practice giving readings as often as you can.

THE MOUNT OF JUPITER (UNDER OR CLOSE TO THE INDEX OR JUPITER FINGER)

The Mount of Jupiter is the most important for assessing strength of character. It signifies ambition, leadership, idealism and wisdom, authority, and altruism (also qualities of the first index Jupiter finger).

- **FIRM, NOT TOO HARD OR SOFT, RISING DIRECTLY UNDER THE FIRST JUPITER FINGER: A wise teacher or mentor, sociable and good in public life, a natural problem-solver and someone who is personally ambitious but fair-minded and cares about those less fortunate.**

- **HOLLOW: A natural follower, ideal for making things happen behind the scenes, may find social interactions hard.**

- **SPONGY AND HIGH: Loves good living, may boast.**

- **VERY LARGE AND HARD: A big ego, eager for professional and social recognition and can be ruthless in seeking power (observe also if the warlike mount of Mars is overdeveloped). Relationships may need hard work or a very compliant partner to survive.**

THE MOUNT OF SATURN (UNDER 2ND OR SATURN FINGER)

The mount of Saturn is concerned with life's problems and coping with them. Generally, this mount is relatively flat, compared with the others, so any prominence suggests someone who has firm boundaries in lifestyle and interactions and the ability to organize efficiently. This mount, along with the corresponding second finger, speaks of a serious, introspective nature, with strong values of right or wrong, hard-working but finding emotions hard and needing self-time; good at law, accountancy, or research.

- **HALFWAY BETWEEN THE JUPITER AND SECOND FINGER:** The best of both qualities.

- **EXCESSIVE OR HARD:** Rigid beliefs, unwillingness to change, dogmatic and stubborn.

- **UNDERDEVELOPED:** Indecisive and fluctuating opinions based on the influence of others.

THE MOUNT OF APOLLO OR THE SUN (UNDER RING OR APOLLO FINGER)

The mount of Apollo and its corresponding ring or third finger is the area of artistic talent of all kinds, creativity, communication skills whether written or spoken, sensitivity, musical talents, a natural performer, good fortune, and scientific or technological ability.

- **IF DIRECTLY BELOW THE APOLLO, THIRD FINGER:** Gifts in and appreciation of arts and culture, a lover of beauty and harmony and with creative tendencies.

- **LARGE AND WELL-DEVELOPED (SIMILAR IN SIZE TO THE JUPITER MOUNT):** Significant success in the arts, luck in games of chance and money-making, especially in an arts or technological-based business.

- **SOFT AND SPONGY:** Charismatic, may be insincere.

- **UNDERDEVELOPED, HOLLOW:** Totally unimaginative, needs facts and figures and guidelines.

THE MOUNT OF MERCURY (UNDER THE LITTLE OR MERCURY FINGER)

The mount of Mercury like the little finger above it, is the area of inventiveness, desire for travel, business and sales acumen, awareness of practical skills, intelligence, versatility, and psychic ability. It involves communication in a factual, as opposed to creative, Apollo sense, persuasiveness, competitiveness, mental alertness, and devotion to family and friends.

Because it is a larger mount than Saturn or Apollo, a similar size would indicate that it was small and under-developed.

- **LARGE, WELL FORMED: The ability to express ideas coherently and effectively, especially in sales or entrepreneurial ventures; also healing abilities, found in those involved in medicine or alternative therapies.**

- **SMALL, UNDERDEVELOPED: Talking especially in public or more than one to one is hard, both professionally and socially.**

- **HOLLOW OR SPONGY: A flatterer, prone to impractical schemes or with delusions of grandeur.**

- **IF DISPLACED BETWEEN THE APOLLO AND MERCURY FINGERS, ESPECIALLY IF BOTH MOUNTS ARE STRONG OR FORMING ONE LARGE SINGLE MOUNT: Innovative ideas, but may need direction; skilled public speaker; entertainer.**

MARS

Mars represents proactive, strong and courageous energies, and sometimes warlike, aggressive tendencies.

There are three main areas associated with Mars on the palm: one main mount, directly under the mount of Mercury, and two areas on the center of the palm forming the Plain of Mars (see diagrams below).

It may be useful to consider this Martian powerhouse as a whole, to see the relative strengths and weaknesses and the overall emphasis.

A strong overall Mars is advantageous, since we all need drive and determination to stand up for our beliefs and to thrive in the world, rather than being downtrodden by others. Teenagers and indeed adults without a strong Mars component may find it hard to stand up against bullying. Those with strong overall Mars may be attracted to security-service careers, in action-packed work, or as campaigners for justice, especially combined with a powerful Jupiter. A powerful but not overdeveloped Mars is also good for business success in a competitive world, or sports.

To easily identify the main upper mount and Plain of Mars, place your fingers of the Inactive hand on the back of your Active hand while applying pressure over your upturned palm with your other thumb. Especially focus on what you feel in energy terms in the different Mars areas.

THE MOUNT OF MARS (DIRECTLY UNDER THE MOUNT OF MERCURY)

The main outer mount of Mars represents physical courage, self-control, desire for action rather than deliberation, and strong passions and the ability to push on regardless of obstacles.

- **IF FLESHY BUT SOFT TO THE TOUCH:** An argumentative nature, but will generally back down if confronted.

- **FIRM AND FLESHY:** Definite unshakeable opinions on every subject.

- **HARD AND OVERDEVELOPED:** Pugnacity and an unwillingness to back away from conflict.

- **IF UNDERDEVELOPED SO YOU CAN HARDLY FEEL IT:** Timidity and gentleness, may have been bullied when young, won't defend own rights or stand against injustice.

- **SPONGY:** Can be sarcastic and critical.

- **LINKED TO THE HEAD LINE:** Excessive nervous energy that can prevent relaxing or switching off mind chatter.

A second inner mount of Mars is also frequently identified just above the mount of Venus within the Life line; generally, if one Mars mount is developed, the other will also be. This second mount especially talks about the ability to stand up for principles and friends and, thus, moral courage. The meanings of the two are very similar.

- **WELL DEVELOPED AND FIRM:** Always eager to do duty, may join organizations when young; a good team leader.

- **OVERDEVELOPED:** Temper tantrums if possessor does not get own way and sometimes unwise behavior to show how tough the person is.

- **UNDERDEVELOPED, FLAT:** Unconventional, won't fit into organizations or play by the rules, prefers to follow own ethics.

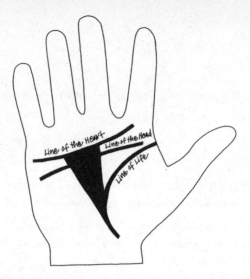

THE PLAIN OF MARS

This is situated in the area of the palm that descends from the center, at the level of the outer mount of Mars, almost to the wrist. The Plain of Mars can be subdivided into Middle Mars, the Quadrangle (so called because of its shape), and Lower Mars (also called the Triangle).

The plain tells us, according to its fleshiness and clear formation, how quickly passions are aroused, sometimes as anger, but more positively as excitement and enthusiasm for new ventures.

- **CRISS-CROSSED WITH FINE RED LINES: Unresolved anger issues, especially if plain is well developed; volatility in close relationships.**

- **FLESHY OR HARD: Easily roused, especially by teasing; vulnerable young people need tactics to deal with this.**

- **UNDERDEVELOPED: An emotional vampire who drains others.**

MIDDLE MARS/THE QUADRANGLE

This lies between the Heart line and the Head line.

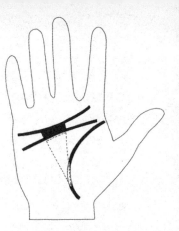

- **IF CLEAR AND WELL FORMED:** Sincerity, protection of the vulnerable, mitigation of the basic warlike aspects of Mars.

LOWER MARS/THE TRIANGLE

This is situated above the mount of Venus which is under the thumb, forming an isosceles triangle downward from the Head line to the Life line. It joins the Quadrangle/Middle Mars.

- **IF CLEAR:** Intellectual achievement using the determination of Mars, also balancing physical and mental energy; physical health and vigor, generosity. Those who have made good after a bad start in life will show strong deep lines on the Triangle.

- **FAINT:** Can have lost incentive to achieve, subject to stress.

THE MOUNT OF THE MOON OR LUNA (UNDER UPPER MARS)

The Mount of the Moon is just above the wrist, forming the second-largest Mount in the average hand (after Venus), and is often quite fleshy, extending to the percussion or edge of the hand.

Mount Luna is formed directly opposite mount Venus and deals with imagination, psychic abilities, past world and predictions/premonitions through enhanced psychometry (information from palms and objects using psychic touch); astral and predictive dreams, and unconscious impulses. More than one area of the hand may express similar qualities, thus enabling a weakness to be counterbalanced, in this case by a clear Intuition line.

- **LARGE AND WELL DEVELOPED:** An active imagination expressed through creative endeavors and spiritual/religious interests; a potential inventor, enjoys travel, happier outdoors, especially by water.

- **SMALL AND SOFT:** Loves routine and familiar places and activities, happiest following directions or instructions rather than improvising.

- **LARGEST MOUNT ON HAND:** A daydreamer who may sometimes lose touch with reality.

THE MOUNT OF VENUS (UNDER THUMB, ACROSS FROM MOON)

This mount is the fount of the human personality; when there are emotional difficulties, it is the one most dramatically affected by circumstances.

It is usually the largest of the mounts, extending from the base of the thumb to the edge of the hand and the wrist.

The mount of Venus, encircled by and empowering the Life line, represents love, passion, including but not exclusively sexual passions, affection, or sentimentality, and is influenced in prominence over time by major changes in relationships, whether romantic, family, or more formal partnerships.

- **IF HIGH, LARGE, AND FLESHY:** Desire for beauty and luxury and the incentive to attain it but can be possessive.

- **IF VERY HIGH AND PROMINENT:** Jealousy, self-indulgence, laziness, sexual excesses, especially if spongy.

- **CRAMPED, HOLLOW, OR COLD TO THE TOUCH:** An absence of sexual desire, perhaps because of a previous hurt, lack of interest in possessions or fine living, may be miserly.

- **IF THE FATE LINE BEGINS ON THE MOUNT OF VENUS:** Strong motivation influenced by family; good at physical activity.

DEVELOPING YOUR READING SKILLS

Now you can start reading in earnest, remembering that it is most helpful if you offer the opportunity at the beginning for people to tell you what they want to know, so you can apply the information in the palm to resolving real-life issues. Mark the mounts on your own diagrams and that of the person whom you have been monitoring closely, and see how this new information modifies or adds to previous findings.

USING A PENDULUM TO FIND AND CLEAR AREAS OF BLOCKAGE, EXCESSES, OR WEAKNESS

This is an extension of the intuitive method that we met in the Introduction: using your hand as a guide to *feeling* the energies. Now we are going to use a pendulum, a crystal on a chain widely available in crystal stores, New Age shops, and online, to tune in to the palm energies and strengthen or calm discordant areas.

We are going to focus primarily on the Active hand initially as the most immediate to positively affect; by working through the palm, you can balance your entire system. You can also later experiment at energizing the Inactive hand and then putting the palms together, as we practiced in the previous chapter.

Why the pendulum? Because if you relax as you pass it over the different lines and mounts on your palm, a few centimeters (an inch or two) above, it will automatically move counterclockwise for as long as necessary to remove any negative palm energies, from side to side to smooth excess energies, and clockwise with varying intensity to strengthen and repair broken or weak lines or mounts.

Use a traditional clear quartz crystal or gentle balancing amethyst pendulum. Hold your pendulum when working on your own energies in your Inactive hand to balance the Active hand, and in your Active hand when working for others.

The beauty of the pendulum method is that you can program the pendulum in advance, by dictating as you move it over a flat surface a few centimeters above, what you would like each directional swing to signify.

Usually the positive swing of a pendulum indicates and inputs energy and activity; stillness in movement, a dead area that will be reactivated by the spontaneous to-and-fro movement of the pendulum to get things going. A blockage is generally indicated by a rushing sensation through your fingers as the pendulum spirals to unravel it; or powerful alternate clockwise and counterclockwise swinging for excess energies, and a reverse swing for a negative or unhelpful energy that needs clearing.

Simply place the palm to be read flat on a table, gently and slowly passing the pendulum over each line and mount in turn, *feeling* the sensations as well as observing the direction of movement. Concentrate on the energies you are feeling, whether a gentle warm tingling or even dead areas in a line or area of the palm where you feel nothing.

Then relax; trust the pendulum if necessary to make a remedial action on that area. When finished, it will simply stop until you move it on to the next area. Top to bottom, left to right over the palm is easiest. Crystals are millions of years old and far wiser than we are, and the amazing thing is that if you trust your pendulum to move in its own way and to make the appropriate movements as long as necessary (you will feel the clearing in your whole system), then the system will move into balance and strong energies will be transferred quite automatically to the appropriate place on the palm—and so to the whole system.

Run the pendulum over the whole hand again, and you may be rewarded by a gently flowing tingling of electricity, as all the aspects move into harmony. This could take up to half an hour; and if problems are deep-set, the whole process may have to be repeated at weekly intervals for a month or more. We will work in Chapter 7 on using a pendulum as part of an integrated palm reading that not only diagnoses but also improves the energies.

PENDULUM PALMISTRY AND PAST LIVES

If you hold your pendulum slowly about an inch over each Mount on your Inactive Hand of Potential, starting with the Mount of Jupiter, you may see images in your mind, *hear* words, or have *strong impressions and memories* of earlier worlds and lives when the energies of that particular mount were predominant. Jupiter may offer flashes of former worlds where you took the lead; Saturn, hard-working lives; Apollo, creative ventures; Mercury, healing and money making; Mars, battles and conflicts; and Venus, love and your Twin Soul and Luna, old ceremonies, and sacred places. Scribble these feelings, images, and words down while you are writing or drawing, and more may come in your dreams in the following nights or in meditation. As you become more practiced and tuned in, you can do this for other people as part of a general psychic consultation as well as add it to your own past life recall. Often, you may discover the origin of a particular fear, and by using one of the palm-healing techniques I have described in the book, you can gradually remove the fear.

In the next chapter, we will examine the all-important thumb and finger significance.

❖ 5 ❖

THE FINGERS
AND THUMBS

TIME TO RECAP. IF YOU ARE FEELING OVER-whelmed by so much information, go back over the previous chapters and identify the main palm features listed in each chapter. For each major feature, *read* the definition of the line or mount, but focus *only* on the characteristics of a well-developed line or mount. Using deduction, you can easily work out from that what an excessive feature would mean and an undeveloped one. Much less to memorize at this stage.

ADDING FINGERS AND THUMBS TO THE PICTURE

Study all the hands you can, and make a quick assessment of their fingers and thumbs, especially if a big person has short, small fingers or a small person has longer, larger ones or prominent ones.

Short fingers indicate an active person who can absorb information rapidly but who wants to achieve everything at once. In contrast, a more patient long-fingered person thinks before speaking or acting.

I am focusing on the fingers and thumbs, especially on the Active hand where the effects of life are most clearly seen. However, you will see differences on the Inactive hand as hand sizes and shapes certainly don't exactly match, any more than individual foot sizes do. Indeed, if you see an issue on the Active hand, looking at the less-developed hand may offer a clue about potentials we are not using or, conversely, where we have gone off-track from the blueprint

Once you consider the fingers and thumbs, you can often instantly see how a weak finger can be compensated for by its mount or indeed a line on the hand that is well developed. If relative finger sizes seem hard to assess because of a low-set thumb or little finger, use a piece of thread or a small ruler to measure finger sizes.

WHERE TO BEGIN

Phalanges (this is the plural of *phalanx*), the three bones of the fingers and thumbs themselves, manifest the energy of their own mount (the thumb is linked to the mount of Venus) and tend to represent, from top (i.e., the tip) to bottom: the first, mental abilities/thought processes/intuitive reasoning; the second, the application of those processes to work, money, and any formal aspects of your life such as study; and the third, all practical everyday matters.

You can assess the amount of energy and area of life in which the energy is manifested, emanating from the mounts, by the relative lengths and sizes of the finger/thumb phalanges, as well as the mount size itself.

A LITTLE BIT OF PALMISTRY

THE FINGERS

Consider the lengths of the fingers in comparison with other fingers, and then assess the relative lengths of the individual finger phalanges.

You may find relative lengths easier to check on the back of the hand. Individual straight fingers are considered ideal.

Jupiter

The pointing finger that indicates what is wanted in life, the Jupiter index finger has the same qualities as the mount of the same name, and strength in one can compensate for weakness in the other. This is true of all four planetary fingers and thumbs with their corresponding mounts.

The Jupiter finger refers to the innate self/personality, ambition, self-confidence, leadership, altruism, authority, and good fortune.

The first Jupiter finger should be approximately the same size as the third Apollo finger, bringing balance, focus, and achievement of realistic aims.

- **A JUPITER FINGER LONGER THAN THE APOLLO FINGER:** A self-starter with powerful drives for worldly success, a natural but benign leader and good teacher/mentor. Watch for excessive lines or markings on the Jupiter finger for potential burnout.

- **EXTRA-LONG, ESPECIALLY IF FLESHY: Can be bombastic.**

- **A JUPITER FINGER SHORTER THAN THE APOLLO FINGER: May go along with others' desires and opinions, especially in career; but in an older person, 50-plus, can

transform this setback into wisdom to know when to act and
when to wait.

- **VERY SHORT JUPITER FINGER, ENDING BELOW THE
  MID-POINT OF THE TOP PHALANX OF THE SATURN
  FINGER:** Pettiness and hiding behind authority figures.

Jupiter Phalanges

- **LONG FIRST PHALANX:** A charismatic leader who
  instinctively knows the right things to do and say to inspire
  others; self-confident and not needing approval of others.

- **LONG SECOND PHALANX:** A forceful leader, very ambitious
  who is unwilling to compromise and less likely to consult others;
  can be selfish if set on what seems the right course.

- **SHORT SECOND PHALANX:** Indicates interest in religion and
  traditional belief systems that grows through the years.

- **LONG THIRD PHALANX:** Successful practical matters in the
  everyday material world, as long as subject does not lose sight of
  original purpose; can be arrogant.

- **SHORT THIRD PHALANX:** Seeks personal happiness rather
  than worldly fulfillment.

Saturn

The second Saturn finger should be the longest finger and is the
finger against which other fingers are measured.

It signifies our acquired character; responsibility; duty; conventional values and ideals; creating boundaries for self and against
others; advancement through slow conventional ways, such as property or safe career; wisdom; and introspection.

- **IF IT IS SIMILAR IN LENGTH TO FINGERS ON EITHER SIDE:** Influenced by the meaning of the other fingers in priorities and values.

- **LONG:** High principles, serious in outlook, rarely relaxes or has fun.

- **SHORT, COMPARED WITH JUPITER 1ST AND APOLLO FINGER 3RD:** Finds taking personal initiative hard, happiest in controlled environment with well-defined rules and set career path.

Saturn Phalanges

- **LONG FIRST PHALANX:** Can be prone to pessimism and mistrust of others.

- **LONG SECOND PHALANX:** A traditional approach to life, good at property deals, very cautious about change; can have superiority complex.

- **LONG THIRD OR BASE PHALANX:** The gardener's phalanx, good at anything to do with the land, animals, wildlife, or gardens.

Apollo

Apollo, the third ring finger, is ideally the same size as the first Jupiter finger. It represents creativity, especially in the arts, desire for fame/recognition in the chosen field, scientific and technological gifts, and luck in money.

- **LONG FINGER, REACHING BEYOND HALF-WAY OF TOP PHALANGE OF SATURN FINGER:** Tendency to take chances in life, often called the Gambler's finger; lucky in business and speculation, happy in own skin, sociable.

- **SHORT FINGER, ENDING BELOW MID-POINT OF TOP PHALANGE OF SATURN:** Prefers to imitate others rather than trusting own ideas, lacks inspiration and drive.

Apollo Phalanges

- **LONGEST TOP PHALANX:** Can reach heights of success creatively, even fame.

- **LONGEST SECOND PHALANX:** Creativity or creative thinking will be beneficial in any career path, natural love of beauty and dislike of messiness in home, charismatic.

- **LONGEST THIRD PHALANX:** Values material success, extravagant, showy possessions and lifestyle, even if gets in debt to achieve.

Mercury

The Mercury little finger is normally parallel with the bottom of the top phalanx of the third finger. Make allowances if Mercury finger is low-set on hand. Use a thread to measure comparative sizes.

The Mercury finger represents persuasiveness in sales, ability to make money, communication through entertaining, dancing, singing, acting or advocacy, business and sales acumen, psychic powers, and healing.

- **LONG FINGER, REACHING THE TOP OR PAST THE FIRST PHALANX OF APOLLO FINGER:** Very confident socially and sexually, gifted in entrepreneurial ventures, tendency to override others' opinions, can have an unconventional streak.

- **SHORT FINGER:** Does not believe in self, constantly searching for happiness and perfection, sexually timid, surprisingly good as a counselor.

- **BENT-OVER:** Attached to/dominated by family, especially parents, in later years can be bullied by children.

- **TWISTED:** Can be liberal with truth, manipulative, prefers sex to love.

Mercury Phalanges

- **FIRST PHALANX GENERALLY LONGEST:** Indicating naturally persuasive with words, salesperson supreme; or, in politics/law, can do well in entertainment.

- **SECOND PHALANX, THE WRITER'S PHALANX:** Can strengthen writer's fork on Head line

- **LARGER THIRD PHALANX:** Good at money-making, business ventures, not always straightforward in financial dealings, better at small talk than meaningful emotions.

Leaning Fingers

Leaning fingers are influenced by those they lean toward.

- **JUPITER FINGER LEANING TOWARD THUMB:** Wants to be in charge of people/situations; if overdeveloped, Jupiter can be totally self-absorbed and selfish.

- **JUPITER LEANING TOWARD SECOND SATURN FINGER:** Seeks support, especially from authority figures; can also indicate co-dependency.

- **SATURN LEANING TOWARD THIRD APOLLO FINGER:** Many interests, but will not test talents in marketplace, can unconsciously sabotage own efforts.

- **APOLLO LEANING TOWARD MERCURY:** Verbally very persuasive, brilliant salesperson; also can be found in natural healers, those who care, and those who give up ambitions to care for sick or disabled family member.

THE THUMB

The thumb represents willpower and motivation, logic, perseverance, and competence. If you can't easily identify the third phalanx, calculate it reaching to the thumb's semi-circular crease on the mount of Venus, usually encircled by Life line.

An average thumb length reaches the middle of the third phalanx of the first Jupiter finger, when you press your thumb to the side of the hand. Use thread to assess comparative lengths if thumbs are low-set on the hands.

- **SET HIGH ON HAND:** A real goer, always ready for adventure and the unusual, including travel.

- **LOW:** Much more cautious about safety and advisability of actions, looks before leaps (if leaps at all).

- **LARGE:** Desperate to win but can ignore consequences of actions.

- **EXCESSIVELY LARGE OR THICK IN COMPARISON WITH THE FINGERS:** Dictatorial and may have issues with anger/self-control if challenged (check with Mars).

- **BULBOUS IN ADDITION TO ABOVE THICKNESS:**
Very volatile and can react in an extreme fashion with little
provocation.

- **SHORT:** More laissez-faire; but if challenged on matters of
personal importance, will dig heels in.

- **UNDERDEVELOPED:** Allows others to dictate life, easily
discouraged.

- **SHORT:** May be underachieving and need encouragement, may
find self-regulation hard; see if other hand is the same.

- **WAISTED:** Sympathetic to others, aware of nonverbal signals.

- **THIN:** Opportunistic and calculating, not given to personal
indulgences.

Thumb Angles and Suppleness of Thumb

Measure the suppleness of the thumb by the first phalange. If the
Inactive hand has a suppler thumb than the Active hand, there is
potential to chill out more.

- **RIGID:** Practical, determined, strong ethics, good with money
but can be unemotional.

- **SUPPLE (GET PERSON TO BEND THUMB):** Generous,
good-natured, but can be naïve toward the intentions of others
and easy-come, easy-go with money.

- **THE WIDER THE ANGLE BETWEEN THUMB AND
JUPITER FINGER:** The more open-hearted, generous,
sometimes overgenerous, rushes in as rescuer where there is
injustice (check Mars also).

- **THUMB USUALLY 45-DEGREE ANGLE TO HAND:** Open-minded, honest and tolerant, but won't be a rebel.

- **NARROW ANGLE:** Focuses on local and family matters, indifferent to wider causes.

- **HIGH-SET THUMB JOINS HAND VERY CLOSE TO FIRST JOINT OF JUPITER FINGER:** Has trouble adapting to new situations or ideas and accepting people or lifestyles that are different.

- **LOW-SET THUMB:** Independent, original thinker, happy to follow own unique life path from relatively early on, can be a rebel.

The Thumb Phalanges

Ideally, the top two phalanges on the thumb, the first representing willpower and the second logic, should be in balance so good ideas are realistic and put effectively into practice.

- **LONG TOP PHALANX:** May display flashes of genius, but risk of mistakes with overhastiness.

- **SHORT:** Would sooner think and dream grandiose plans than do them.

- **LONG SECOND PHALANX:** Wise and diligent, thinks and plans everything through but can overthink and put obstacles in own way with problems that might never happen.

- **WAISTED:** Natural diplomat and negotiator.

- **SHORT:** Goes ahead with plans without thinking them through.

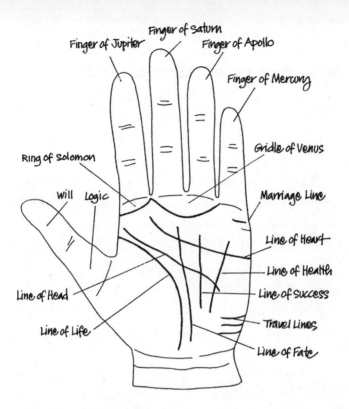

The third phalanx ends on the mount of Venus and is the source of vitality and well-being and of relating to people's needs.

- **FULL AND FIRM:** Sign of good health, an affectionate sociable nature, puts other people higher than personal gain.

- **OVERDEVELOPED WITH SHORT FIRST AND SECOND PHALANGES:** Strong sexual desires.

- **ABSENT BECAUSE OF HOLLOW MOUNT OF VENUS:** Finds it hard to synthesize logic with feelings and so may find people's reactions puzzling. Can seem somewhat like a person who has Asperger's.

DEVELOPING YOUR READING SKILLS

The more aspects you learn about the hand, the more you may find seeming contradictions. Don't fear you are reading inaccurately. We are all full of contradictions that often represent inner conflicts, and discussion during the reading can resolve these.

Once you have marked and assessed information on your original diagrams about your own fingers and thumbs and for the person with whom you have been working closely, you will be ready to write a profile of your findings.

In the meantime, keep trying to match casual thumb and finger assessments in daily life to what you know/can discover about the people you observe.

Start with your own Active hand's profile, and you can create a template that will be useful for future readings. You can add the second hand in exactly the same way when we develop profiling in Chapter 7, and by adding with the markings and lesser lines from Chapter 3.

CREATING A BASIC PROFILE

Print a new blank Active hand diagram and add features as you go.

This first profile may take a while, so use your own hand or that of the person who has been cooperating, so you can add the info in the order below and then check it at your leisure. But once you are palm reading in detail, you will whizz through it using intuition if the facts elude you. You can work from the diagrams of the Active hand that you have already created, but it may be easier to build up a new picture using just the headings below.

For ease, we are going to use only the four major lines from Chapters 1 and 2 and a few subsidiary ones, plus any salient lines such as marriage or children lines if those are an issue in the reading (Chapter 3), then the mounts (Chapter 4), fingers, and thumbs.

Although in the next chapter we will add the other lines and markings to our profile, if you prefer, you can always use this basic one and just study and add relevant lines, such as travel, where questions relate to them.

Create a shorthand, for example a hill image for a well-developed mount or an inverted hill for a hollow mount; and you can draw arrows to indicate where one finger leans toward another.

Gain information while we are practicing from the line and mount definitions, flipping through the book to check the different basic definitions. Take your time.

So, magnifying glass at the ready? Look at the hand picture higher up in this chapter to guide you to the most likely positions of the relevant lines listed below and to the diagrams of individual mounts and so forth in the earlier chapters. For each line, mount, etc., on your profile, scribble under the heading (leave plenty of space under each entry) any significant features, any strengths and potential pitfalls.

The Profile Sheet

This can be written or printed and, if you wish, you can create a template for your Active hand.

Name:

Age:

Any special questions/issues that the reading could answer:

The Lines:

>Heart line
>
>Head line
>
>Life line
>
>Fate or Destiny line
>
>Sun or Apollo line
>
>Health line
>
>Intuition line (optional)
>
>Relationship/Marriage and Children lines if relevant
>
>*Any significant interactions formed by these lines:*

The Mounts:

>Mount of Jupiter
>
>Mount of Saturn
>
>Mount of Apollo
>
>Mount of Mercury
>
>Mount and Plain of Mars
>
>Mount of Luna or the Moon
>
>Mount of Venus
>
>Any significant interaction between individual lines and mounts.

Fingers and Thumb:

    Thumb

    Jupiter, first or index finger

    Saturn, second finger

    Apollo, third or ring finger

    Mercury, little finger

    Any significant interaction between individual thumb, fingers, and mounts to which they relate.

Summary of strengths and weaknesses of the whole hand (Suggested action/improvements/changes in lifestyle related to the whole hand, to answer questions posed by the subject (remedies based on discussion with subject)*:*

In the next chapter, we will learn about the significance of markings on the hand.

❖ 6 ❖

THE MARKINGS
ON THE PALMS

THE MARKINGS ON THE PALMS ARE PRONE TO
change over relatively short periods, when there has been
an alteration in lifestyle or circumstances (sometimes
influenced by a palm reading that puts life in perspective). These
markings are especially positively influenced by pendulum healing
and in using your palm stone or pressing your hands together to balance energies. Using a magnifying glass is the best way to examine
the markings.

On the whole, there are more markings on the Active hand,
but those on the Hand of Potential can represent unresolved past
life matters, potential weaknesses, or indeed untapped strengths in
this lifetime that can be modified or activated once recognized. For
example, the already-mentioned fork at the end of the Head line, the
Writer's fork, the mark of the writer and communicator, can appear
on the hand of Potential as a dream yet to be awakened.

So too on the Active hand, the same signs may appear along the length of the line, in past, present, and future. Maybe a parent has always interfered with or discouraged you and is still doing so whenever you have wanted to make a major change or resolve a sticking point, and the markings will disappear over time.

Though I describe each of the markings separately, they will always have the most significance in relation to the lines, mounts, or areas of the palm they cross or cover. Despite some gloomy old-fashioned palmistry books, death, disaster, or serious illness are never predicted in the hand, though markings may suggest that you should take more care of yourself.

UNDERSTANDING THE MARKINGS

Markings can be both positive and negative and indicate a blockage, interruption, or sometimes additional source of power on a line or mount. Markings are best initially *felt* with the hand or pendulum to see if they are dead energy, a tangle, or a build-up of power. You can then talk about their significance and offer a bit of pendulum healing if appropriate. Look at other strengths in the hands that can offer positive resources to get things moving and turn challenge to opportunity.

Chains

CHAINS, JOINED CIRCLES: Obstacles you are facing/have faced (especially as past-life conflict on the non-Active hand).

- **HEART LINE CHAINS:** If in the past on the Active hand, earlier setbacks in love that you have not fully resolved; if ongoing, current relationship concerns that need dealing with.

- **A DEEP CHAIN COVERING THE PRESENT AREA OF THE HEART LINE:** Overemotional/possessive connections or even co-dependency.

- **ANY HEAVILY CHAINED LINES:** Energy draining away, a lifestyle change, reduction of stress, a healthier diet, or gentle exercise may help.

- **HEAD LINE WITH CHAINS:** Many alternative directions and distractions from life path, having too many projects going at once, completing none satisfactorily.

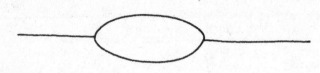

Islands

Islands, ovals that may be single or recurring, indicate unfavorable interruptions in life. If ahead, see how forward planning can avert. But sometimes an island indicates the need for leisure, self-time, or reprioritizing.

- **ON LIFE LINE:** Daily stress or depression.

- **ON FATE LINE:** Money worries that may have built up over a period.

- **ON HEART LINE IF REGULAR:** Unresolved emotional issues from childhood (see if they start near the beginning), creating trust or commitment issues in later relationships.

- **AN ISLAND OR MORE ON JUPITER:** A previous setback in ambitions that should not deter future efforts, consider alternative strengths such as a powerful finger of Jupiter or thumb that may offer new resources.

- **A SINGLE ISLAND ON THE MOUNT OF VENUS:** Temptation to have an affair, an indication of discontentment in an existing relationship.

- **BRAIDED ISLANDS:** Looking like embroidery—building up of family tensions, maybe over years—worth spending time talking about, maybe healing.

Worry Lines
- **NUMEROUS FINE LINES MAINLY, FROM BASE OF THUMB TOWARD LIFE LINE, EVEN CROSSING IT BUT CAN BE FOUND ON OTHER PARTS OF PALM:**
  If on Potential hand, indicates a natural worrier, needing more relaxation, meditation to avoid burnout by worrying about what may never happen.

Squares

Squares on the Life line are positive, mitigating any less-than-positive signs they are near.

Especially lucky after a triangle, a square amplifies the strengths and good fortune of its mount or line, a virility/fertility symbol especially on the mounts of Venus and Luna/the Moon.

- **AROUND THE MOON MOUNT OR THE INTUITION LINE:**
  The close presence of your Guardian angel or Spirit Guide; if in the future, finding the right mentor or guru or becoming one yourself.

- **ON OR AROUND THE JUPITER MOUNT:** A gifted conventional teacher or facilitator of workshops or courses on personal interest/alternative therapies.

Crosses

Despite their name, crosses can have positive meanings, heralding major changes where results, even if initially disruptive, open new opportunities.

Less positively (*feel* the energies), crosses signify outside influences that can be causing stress, someone or something railroading you into a decision. If a cross *feels* heavy, talk about what is causing doubts. Maybe it's not what you want deep down, even to keep the peace.

- **ON THE JUPITER MOUNT: Readiness for new experiences, especially if there is a restrictive grille marking nearby.**

- **THE MYSTIC CROSS, AN UPRIGHT CROSS BETWEEN THE HEAD AND HEART LINES: Gifts in the psychic arts/ therapies and, if wished, a career in them.**

Grilles

Grilles tend to be found on mounts rather than lines, representing the need for freedom in an area of your life where you often hit a brick wall. Identifying and overcoming a grille releases energy and frees you from an old attitude or pattern or a person who deters you from traveling or trying new things. Grilles are very responsive to pendulum healing.

- **IF GRILLES APPEAR ALL OVER THE PALM: Take a step back and see who or what is causing an energy leak or annoyance.**

Dots or Spots

Dots appear in a row anywhere on the palm and are filled in, different from chains or islands. Especially if worry lines are present, they represent *worries* about health or fears about job loss or relationship failure. They do not predict disasters, but ask what grounds there are for the fears: whether, for example, fear of infidelity comes from past letdowns or whether there is behavior around you that gives rise to valid fears. Whatever the fear, a health check if you have symptoms you are ignoring, a discussion with personnel at work instead of listening to rumors, or an honest talk with a partner generally causes the dots to disappear.

Stars

Stars on the palm indicate success and good fortune in the area/mount/line where they appear, enhancing the strengths represented by the lines or mounts. The only drawback is if people have it too easy and don't push themselves or settle for second best.

- **STARTING AFTER A STAR:** Great accomplishments, but a long road.

- **ENDING A LINE:** Total success, often involving travel, even fame.

- **ON THE MOUNT OF THE MOON:** A sign of celebrity and media success.

- **ON THE MOUNT OF JUPITER OR SATURN:** High profile, achievements in public office.

Tassels

- **TASSELS OR FRAYED LINES:** Temporary confusion, or an impasse linked to the relevant line or mount. They can disappear rapidly once the confusion is cleared; step back if the chaos is coming from someone else.

Triangles

Lucky, heralding success in the area of the palm or on the lines where they are found, especially in multitasking and when more than one opportunity presents itself.

- **ON THE MOUNTS OF SATURN OR THE MOON:** Psychic and healing powers that may lead to a media career if chosen.

- **ON THE SUN/APOLLO OR MERCURY MOUNTS:** A razor-sharp mind, promising financial, scientific, or business success and recognition, even internationally.

- **A SMALL TRIANGLE RIGHT IN THE CENTER OF THE PALM:** The ability to earn money through your own abilities.

- **A CLOSED MONEY TRIANGLE:** Money will be easily conserved.

- An open money triangle: You may spend a lot but can earn well too.

- A second triangle inside the first: Investing the money in property or shares will bring long-term dividends.

Great Triangle

A more permanent marking created by the conjunction of the Life, Head, and Fate or Health lines, a sign of lifetime success.

- **IF WIDE:** Breadth of vision and lateral thinking.
- **IF NARROWLY ANGLED:** Conventional thinking and traditional beliefs.

Tridents

- **A TRIDENT ANYWHERE ON THE PALM:** A luck-bringer for health, wealth, and happiness, generally enhancing the qualities of lines and the hands.
- **A TRIDENT POINTING DOWN:** Don't let opportunity drain away or take good luck for granted.

READING THE PALM BY ADDING THE MARKINGS

Once you have learned the significance of the markings, run your pendulum or your Active hand (or your Inactive hand if studying your own Active hand) a few centimeters above each of the lines and mounts to feel the intensity and positivity of the markings. Impressions, images, and words will come spontaneously into your mind.

Complete your own hand prints and those of the person with whom you are working closely by adding the markings to the diagrams you have already started. Note how the markings amplify or negate the energies of the related mounts and lines. Since you have added to each hand using the information in each chapter, you can make comparisons of how potential and actual relate.

With all readings involving markings, be doubly sure to date the readings, since three months further on, some will have disappeared or changed. Modify the energies of the mount/line or whole area.

One example would be those fine red lines you noted on the plain of Mars that signified anger. If so, run your fingers or pendulum over the whole Mars area. Are the energies generally over-harsh? Check the inactive Mars area on the hand of Potential to see if the potential for anger is an innate family trait or caused by circumstances, such as bad experiences or unfair treatment and so present only on the Active hand.

Conversely, is the potential for anger on the Potential/Inactive hand, but being suppressed on the Active Hand, when you might expect chains or grilles (thus bad for health)? More positively, is it being channeled into activity and achievement through a nearby square or triangle?

Equally, if there are markings on any of the mounts of the Potential hand, are they present on the Active hand, or have they been supplanted by life's experiences or waiting for the right time to emerge, especially if lucky?

Healing or Modifying Markings

You can use the hand-pressing method in Chapter 3, the palm stone or the pendulum to transfer energy from the Inactive to the Active hand, or draw off excesses and strengthen weaknesses.

As I suggested in Chapter 4, you can use a pendulum, counter-clockwise, to untangle; diagonally, to smooth energies if overactive; and clockwise, to energize, specifically on markings as well as the rest of the palm if any feel negative or blocked.

Hold the pendulum a few centimeters (an inch or two) above each troublesome marking and allow it to move in its own way for as long as necessary. You can easily teach clients to do this.

Also, use rose or lavender oil to gently massage the markings, as well as any problematic lines or mounts. Since the palms are power-fully linked to your overall energy field, especially through the Heart energy center, you can intervene positively to harmonize the whole-body energies. You will feel the relief in your system and new solutions suggesting themselves. Though you may primarily work with the Active hand, massaging the Potential Inactive hand can help to release unused potential.

Creating an Expanded Profile

Until you become totally automatic at profiling, let's monitor just the Active hand, though of course you can, as mentioned above, make comparisons with the Inactive hand if you want to check something, such as when a marking first appeared or if an underdeveloped mount has always been that way. Sketch in any branches or breaks.

Again, use your magnifying glass, even with a printout of a digital camera image. Talk spontaneously, entering into dialogue with the subject as you go.

Print a new Active blank hand (reduced in size) and set it at the top of the profile so you can draw in the relevant features as well as write.

Now add the extra lines and markings listed on page 93, both to the diagram at the top and to the expanded written headings. Once more, create your own shorthand to indicate hollow mounts or unusual activity, etc. If a listed line is absent, note this and what you see as the significance.

THE PROFILE SHEET:

This can be written or printed (*leave plenty of space between categories for comments*).

Name:

Age:

Any special questions/issues that the reading could answer:

The Lines:

- **Heart line**

- **Head line**

- **Life line**

- **Fate or Destiny line**

- **Sun or Apollo line**

- **Health line, sometimes called the Hepatica or Mercury line**

- **Intuition line (optional)**

- **The line of Mars**

- **The line of Money**

- **Travel lines**

- **Ring or Girdle of Venus**

- **Ring of Solomon**

- **Via Lascivia**

- **Relationship/Marriage and Children lines if relevant**

- **Any significant interactions formed by these lines**

The Mounts

- **Mount of Jupiter**

- **Mount of Saturn**

- **Mount of Apollo**

- **Mount of Mercury**

- **Mounts and plain of Mars**

- **Mount of Luna or the Moon**

- **Mount of Venus**

Rascettes (Bracelet lines on the inner wrist immediately below the palm):

- **Bracelet 1: Health, closest to the palm**

- **Bracelet 2: Prosperity**

- **Bracelets 3 and 4: Authority and status**

- **Any significant interaction between individual lines and mounts:**

- **Fingers and Thumb**

- **Thumb**

- **Jupiter, first/index finger**

- **Saturn second finger**

- **Apollo/third/ring finger**

- **Mercury, little finger**

- **Any significant interaction between individual Thumb, Fingers, and mounts to which they relate**

Markings (sketch these individually as well as on the handprint and add comments):

Summary of strengths and weaknesses of the whole hand:

Suggested action/improvements/changes in lifestyle related to the whole hand, to answer questions posed by the subject (remedies based on discussion with subject):

In the final chapter, we will put everything together.

PUTTING IT ALL TOGETHER: DETAILED PALM READING

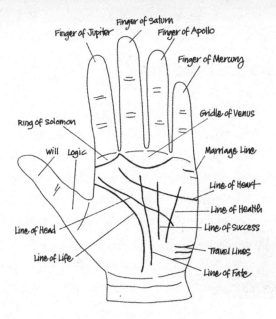

Finger of Saturn
Finger of Jupiter
Finger of Apollo
Finger of Mercury
Ring of Solomon
Girdle of Venus
Will   Logic
Marriage Line
Line of Heart
Line of Health
Line of Head
Line of Success
Line of Life
Travel Lines
Line of Fate

A S YOU READ PALMS, YOU ARE CONNECTING with ancient traditions. Prehistoric hand prints with magical significance have been found on cave walls in places as far apart as France and Africa and Aboriginal Australia, the latter extending back to 40,000 BCE or earlier. Palmistry as a divinatory art is believed by many scholars to have originated in India more than 4,500 years ago and traveled from India into China via trade routes and thence westward to Egypt and Ancient Greece.

A book titled *Physiognomy & Palmistry* was written by Pythagoras, the Ancient Greek philosopher and mathematician, between about 582 BCE and 497 BCE. It is recorded that Aristotle as well as the Roman emperors Augustus and Julius Caesar were skilled in palmistry.

PUTTING IT ALL TOGETHER

Once you feel ready, start reading palms for friends, family, and acquaintances. How formal and detailed your palmistry readings are is entirely up to you and may vary according to the needs of the subject. Sometimes this will be a fun, five- or ten-minute assessment of one or both hands, a quick appraisal of the Active hand to answer a specific question with brief comparison of untapped potential in the other hand, or for an hour and a half if you are making formal profiles for each hand if there are major life-path changes and then putting your conclusions together (simply add *Overall Conclusions and Recommendations* to the end of the Active hand printout).

INTUITIVE PALM READING

In practice, many palm readings will answer specific questions, rather than a full-scale life path, and do not need recording. But have lots of preprinted blank palms/profile sheets, just in case.

Before doing a reading if you don't feel very confident, return to the diagram at the start of the chapter and mark in red the main lines and mounts, plus maybe travel, children, and marriage relationship lines if relevant.

Now go back to chapters 1, 2, 3, and 5, and for each major area of the hand scribble a few words on a Reminder Sheet for the meanings of the main lines and mounts. If in doubt, apply common sense as to meanings. Remember, a wavy or pale line is clearly not as dynamic as a strong deep one. Re-read your checklist and diagram until you are familiar with positions and basic meanings. The hand of Potential is simply the other way around. You will soon acquire an instant feel for what is relevant to consider in a reading. With practice, you will be adding all you have learned—fingers, thumbs, and markings, and the subtler lines and rings—although you will not necessarily need to consider them all except in a life review.

Begin a reading with intuitive sensing of energies, even when you are confident of all the hand meanings. Keep talking. Dialog is the key.

- Move your fingers or pendulum slowly and gently on or very close to the lines and mounts of the Active hand, starting with Heart, Head, Life, and Destiny; then move to any other lines/ mounts that you consider relevant. To recap, the positive swing of a pendulum indicates energy and activity, stillness a blockage, a rushing sensation through your fingers or powerful alternate clockwise and counterclockwise swinging for excess energies, and a counterclockwise swing for negative energies.

- Concentrate on the energies you are feeling, whether a gentle warm tingling, a blockage, or dead areas in a line or area of the palm where you feel nothing, and assess the intensity on a 1-to-10 scale.

- If the palm is criss-crossed by the gently flowing tingling of electricity, all the aspects are in harmony.

- Blockages can indicate a temporary obstacle, which can sometimes be self-imposed or can indicate a period of necessary waiting. Your instinct will tell you which. A blockage is a potential source of energy for change.

- If areas feel dead or more positively temporarily asleep, ask yourself and the subject why. It can indicate that a particular avenue, for example in career or love, has ended in the heart or mind, if not in actuality; or that a bad experience has led to a lack of trust or confidence and so talents and feelings have atrophied. This is not a once-and-for-all state and can, given encouragement, revive.

- Put down the pendulum and study visually through your magnifying glass the relative strength, length, and continuity of the lines.

- Is the person's current emphasis in the area of Head or Heart, and does the life line offer a store of energy or indicate exhaustion and anxiety? You can check what you feel as well as see anywhere on the Active hand, on the corresponding Potential hand to see what resources are available to be manifested in the Active hand. Alert the subject.

- Which mounts are prominent and/or undeveloped? Why? Is this different on the Potential hand?

- Are there many marks and/or distinctive lines for travel or family? Are these interconnected?

- What is absent in the Active hand that was present in the Potential hand that could potentially aid the subject? Have forks in the Potential not yet been pursued? Has a potentially strong or developed mount of the Moon with its intuitive strengths on the Inactive hand or a powerful Head line been neglected in the real world so that these potential strengths are not being utilized?

- What suggestions for future action can be made from the combination of potential and actuality?

- Keep a copy of the palm drawings, and in three or six months take new images. You will be surprised at the changes.

RELATIONSHIP READING FOR COUPLES

Ask each person separately what they most want to know. Each may have a totally different perspective on their lives and future. Initially, separate readings for couples may be easier unless they are young and totally in love, but you can follow with a shorter joint session in which you can show each the compatibilities and differences in their respective hands and use this as a basis for making joint resolutions, perhaps using a blue pen to mark over the complementary lines on the diagrams, and red or black for differences.

Couples don't need total compatibility, but be aware if one person has very dominant features and the other gentler. This may suit them, as even twin souls should not mirror, but complement. A strong Head line in one partner may go well with a strong Heart line in the other, whereas two strong Head or Fate lines can bring issues with dominance, or one being very pale and wavy and the other deep and grooved can indicate a bullying partner. If one of the parties is newly divorced, there may be lots of grilles and chains remaining on the Heart line where an ex-partner is still exerting a pull, even if the original relationship is broken. Problematic in-laws can be similarly featured, especially if they preferred an ex-partner to the present one. Braided islands indicate family tensions that can adversely affect a love relationship.

Relationship/Marriage lines, the fine lines that extend slightly diagonally across the side of the palm between the start of the Heart line and the Mercury finger, should also be compared, as these will hold crucial information. The longest line is the current relationship and should be clear and well-marked, coming from the side of the hand and on to the surface of the palm. If the line is absent, short, or broken, have a look at the Heart line of the person with the fractured connection, especially for any markings that might indicate outside interference or a frozen heart. Also check the mount of Venus on both hands if the Active one is hollow.

Note the appearance of the individual relationship lines. For example, a troubled relationship will often be reflected as a fragmented, jagged, or wavering line. A love line that is forked could indicate a *potential* parting of the ways, but this can be averted with tact and care. In such cases, counseling will be part of the reading or should be recommended.

A deeper groove is usually a solid sign of a strong-lasting bond despite difficulties.

Look at the Children lines too if relevant, fine vertical lines immediately below the Mercury finger, sometimes overlapping the Marriage/Relationship lines. Compare their strength or waviness if there are major custody problems or if there are plans for future joint children—or, indeed, in a childless couple if one is reluctant (very pale, absent, or not crossing or touching the marriage lines). In a newly married couple, check the Children lines of existing children. The Children lines may branch off a relationship line indicating that children are an issue, especially if from a previous relationship, and watch out for a grille or island on the line of the birth parent.

Existing children will have stronger longer lines than potential ones.

If you are doing a reading for both people at the same time, go from Active hand to Active hand for each feature, and if seemingly insurmountable problems become apparent, look to the early parts of the Heart line and Venus mount on the hand of Potential for the very factors that may have attracted them in the first place. The younger the couple, the more significant the hand of Potential.

READING FOR TEENAGERS OR AT A PARTY

This is a fun activity whether at a teenage sleepover or the office party. Everyone present photographs and prints out digital-camera images of their own Active hand, picks a number out of a hat and writes the number on the back of the sheet, mixes them up, and each person takes one to interpret, without knowing the identities. Buy small magnifying glasses for each person.

Have a big printout or individual diagram/s of the basic hand, marking the following key lines in red pen.

Create also a large check sheet, for Heart, Head, Life, Fate, or Destiny, Apollo Sun line for Fame and Fortune, Money line, mount of Venus for Love and Moon for Psychic powers, with a few words of meaning for each (or you can print these out separately, one for each person), plus Children, Relationship, and Travel lines. The reader scribbles the findings on the printout. Afterwards, each person identifies their number as the results are read out one by one.

You can also ask people to bring a printout of their boyfriend/girlfriend's Active hand, and everyone passes them around in turn, adding to the group interpretation. If an office party, you can add the Jupiter and Saturn mounts for career.

A CASE STUDY

Susanne, a single parent from London, has been laid off from her job as a graphic designer; and because she has little help with her young daughter, she is very limited as to the work she can take on and debts are mounting. What options, if any, are open to her? I focused mainly on her Active hand, but checked also with the hand of her Potential to answer her pressing questions.

The most significant feature was the broken and deeply indented Fate line that was scattered with grilles and islands. Her loss and fears for the future had clearly made their mark. The island indicates her isolation by her job loss, but also ironically sanctuary from the previously exhausting pressures of struggling to travel and take care of her child while working full-time.

Already, however, her Apollo/creative fortune line is starting to branch toward her Head and Fate lines in the direction of the mounts of Saturn and Apollo, promising that her creative side will offer her a way out of her problems.

Very faintly she has, on the mount of the Moon, a triangle indicating psychic and healing powers and an even fainter Mystic Cross between the Head and Heart lines, and a reasonably well developed but not pulsating mount of the Moon, all signs of psychic gifts. Susanne told me she had always been gifted in psychic arts but had never developed them. I checked on her Potential hand, and there were both triangles quite clearly, waiting to be activated.

Since Susanne is qualified as a graphic designer, all this is pointing to the fact that she could combine her gifts and design New Age websites as a business and offer her own psychic services on her website—and this business she can do anywhere. A well-developed Mercury mount on her Active hand promises that her existing versatility and ingenuity will see her through; and, with its money-making and technological associations, it would seem that Susanne can succeed in specialist web designing.

But most significant and unexpected to me were the Travel lines on both hands that were clearest on her Potential hand. Travel lines are fine lines which can be both vertical and horizontal, starting vertically from the edge of the palm at the base and coming up toward the mount of the Moon on the little finger Mercury side of the hand. They were clearly formed, indicating opportunities to live and work or even emigrate overseas. But where? I asked Susanne if relocation was possible, especially as London was so expensive. While she had considered designing websites, though not connected with the psychic till I showed her the psychic marks, Susanne had been worried about paying her mortgage while getting established as a website designer.

But as a website designer in an area where there is much demand for technological expertise in setting up psychic businesses, that was much more of a possibility. Susanne said her parents owned a cottage in France, next to their converted farmhouse, and when her relationship broke up they had offered it rent-free. But she had not been sure if she could make a go of website work until now that she saw her specialist niche. What is more, if she ran her business from France she could sublet her small London apartment and so have a small nest egg for the future.

When I heard from Susanne six months later, she had moved to France with her daughter and was already getting work, not only as a web designer for New Age websites—there *was* a huge demand—but she was making even more money managing the websites on behalf of her clients. Susanne was doing tarot readings and her other love (previously abandoned passion), astrology, for the numerous expatriates and online. Her daughter was benefiting greatly from daily contact with her grandparents, who lived next door.

Often a palm reading will confirm the validity of half-formed plans dismissed as impractical by revealing strengths and possibilities not considered, sometimes resting in the hand of Potential.

BABIES AND PALMISTRY

A newborn baby has clearly defined Life, Heart, Head, and Fate or Destiny lines, plus other palm lines such as the creative Apollo line, as their basic blueprint; and an Intuition Line if the infant from the beginning smiles at angels, fairies, and deceased ancestors. The two hands are remarkably similar in the early stages of life.

Even in the first weeks, you can see if a Head (logical thinking) line is stronger, longer, and deeper than the Heart/Emotions line and if the baby has a powerful creative line. These early trends represent your baby's potential; and if every six months you study how the lines are developing, you can monitor your child's evolving Active Hand (the differences in palm lines should be clearer from two to three years old onwards). You can discover if a bit more creative input is needed, if the little one would benefit from extra stories to bring the imagination out and/or is ready to play with counting toys. A strong-willed proactive child will have a powerful Fate or Destiny line. The Life line represents all the stored energy (extra-hungry babies may have very defined ones) and an active infant will continue to manifest a strong Life line throughout childhood. Indeed, with plenty of outdoor activities over the years, the Active hand Life line will continue to flourish. You may see competitive tendencies in a straight Fate line aiming for the Jupiter finger even from the first. However, it may be that future generations, with the emphasis on technological stimulation, will have much stronger Head lines and Mercury mounts than in earlier times.

As your child grows, you may discover that those early trends still form the basic blueprint. Keep the first digital-camera images of the palms in the baby's memory box.

PALMISTRY IN YOUR LIFE

Palmistry is the easiest and most portable form not only of divination, but for life planning, and it fits excellently with counseling, mentoring, and life coaching, as well as understanding friends and family and your own hidden strengths and challenges.

So, enjoy this book, take what you will from it, and maybe return to the finer details once you are confidently interpreting palm energies intuitively. If you are a healer, you may wish to include palm healing in more general healing processes.

We make our own Destiny. Nothing is fixed; but with the life map of your palms, you can plan the route and avoid obstacles on your pathway—and above all, explore the wonderful treasury of potential still waiting to be unfolded.

—CASSANDRA EASON, *April 2018*

INDEX

ABOUT THE AUTHOR

Cassandra Eason is an international author and broadcaster on all aspects of crystals, folklore, Celtic wisdom, Wicca, sacred sites, earth energies, divinations, and natural magic. She has studied palmistry for over twenty-five years, and has taught people internationally to interpret and heal through palmistry. Cassandra has published over eighty books on different aspects of healing, magick, divination, and energy work, including *The Complete Crystal Handbook* and *A Spell a Day*.